Education in the Information Age

What Works and What Doesn't

Claudio de Moura Castro
Editor

Inter-American Development Bank

Editorial Manager: Susan Baird Kanaan
Designer: Tom Suzuki
Assistant Designer: Yun K. Pak
Typeset in Dante with Display type in BankA-Normal
Printed and bound by Automated Graphics Systems

**Cataloging-in-Publication data provided by the
Inter-American Development Bank
Felipe Herrera Library**

Seminar on Education in the Information Age (1997 : Cartagena, Colombia)

Education in the information age : what works and what doesn't/
Claudio de Moura Castro, editor.
p. cm.
Includes bibliographical references.
ISBN: 1-886938-33-4
1. Educational technology—Congresses. 2. Education—Data processing—
Congresses. 3. Computer-assisted instruction—Congresses. 4. Distance
education—Congresses. I. Castro, Claudio de Moura. II. Inter-American
Development Bank. III. Title.
371.3078 S36—dc20

ACKNOWLEDGMENTS

This book would not have been possible without the effort of many people. Our deepest thanks for their dedication and competence.

Sandra Bartels played an important role in the organization of the Cartagena Seminar which originated the present book.

Warren Buhler believed in the event and made it bigger and better.

Peter Knight was instrumental in identifying and interacting with participants, in order to give the requisite focus and content to the event.

Laurence Wolff has given valuable advice in putting together the manuscript.

Education
in the
Information Age

Contents

I. The Challenges of Bringing Technology to Education /15/

II. The Unfinished Agenda: Computers in Academic Schools /83/

III. The Success Stories: The Use of Distance Education /131/

Appendices /202/

Foreword

eword

We are pleased to present a timely book about the use of technology in education. By publishing this volume we are expressing the Inter-American Development Bank's belief in the potential for learning offered by information technologies. Indeed, the IDB believes that the judicious use of these technologies can help bridge the gap separating mature education systems from the diverse but collectively disappointing education systems of Latin America and the Caribbean.

Technology is not a magic solution, however. Not everything works. Nothing is easy. There are no "push-button" solutions. To be effective, specific technology must be carefully matched to the need and the environment.

These two principles—the promise of technology and the need for caution and care in its application—combined with a desire to know what works and what doesn't were the guiding themes for a lively seminar in Cartagena in July 1997. The event, organized by the IDB and the Global Information Infrastructure Commission, was called *Education in the Information Age.*

The seminar engaged an impressive list of names from the ranks of academia, schools, business and government. Despite their different biographies and affiliations, they had one thing in common: They are seasoned practitioners, having spent many years trying to use technology in education. They spoke about their own experience. They tried to distill for participants the lessons learned. They sorted out what works and what does not work.

Their collective experience warrants a cautious optimism toward technology—or what one participant called the "mindful use of technology." Of course, the old truths about technological education still apply: namely, that success depends not just on the judicious choice of technology but equally on addressing the stubborn factors that make all social change and organizational reform arduous.

Importantly, the seminar was an occasion to reinforce our assumption that we are not alone in this expedition. Support from the private sector is not only vital for success but also manifestly present. The participants witnessed concrete examples of commitment from the representatives of large and small enterprises during the seminar, and we are led to believe that much more is on the way.

We trust that our readers will find this book a useful contribution to their thinking and learning.

STEPHEN A. QUICK
Manager, Strategic Planning and
Operational Policy Department, IDB

WALDEMAR F.W. WIRSIG
Manager, Sustainable Development
Department, IDB

Education in the Information Age
Lessons from the Seminar

T his book reports the experience of practitioners who have put information technology to use in education. They have learned lessons and are practicing the art in many parts of the world. The seminar in which this book originated was

Stephen A. Quick
Claudio de Moura Castro

not about new ideas or theoretical formulations but rather about the more pedestrian but often more arduous task of asking what works and what does not work. Some common threads emerge, and the present essay tries to capture them.

The global economy is currently undergoing an information revolution whose significance will equal that of the Industrial Revolution of the 19th Century. At that moment, having coal and iron ore and the ability to harness them in steel mills was the critical step. Using this raw material to build better looms and spinning machines established the comparative advantages which put some European countries ahead of the rest of the world.

At present (in the words of Peter Drucker), "the comparative

Stephen A. Quick is the Manager of the Strategic Planning and Operational Policy Department of the Inter-American Development Bank.

Claudio de Moura Castro is Chief Education Advisor in IDB's Sustainable Development Department.

advantage that counts is the application of knowledge.... This means, however, that developing countries can no longer expect to base their development on low wages. They, too, must learn to base development on applying knowledge."

Clearly, applying knowledge to everyday business means that the people working in this business must understand and master the requisite technologies. This requires creating a labor force that is capable of dealing with information technology.

POINTS OF CONSENSUS AT THE SEMINAR

The seminar participants were in agreement about the following points:

1. *It is imperative to transform the nature of education toward building higher-order cognitive skills, more inquiry and project-focused modes of operation, and more collaborative working styles, and toward creating "smart learners."*

2. *Information technology can play an important role in the process of educational change: by opening access to a wealth of information, by facilitating the process of inquiry and by engaging the interest and attention of the learner.*

TV, CD-ROMs and the Internet open the doors to an immense trove of information. Access eventually will be easy and inexpensive (once the fixed costs of equipment and connection are dealt with). There is ample agreement on the ability of these media to charm users and increase their attention span.

3. *"Technological fluency" may stand alongside reading and mathematics as one of the essential skills for a successful life.*

Word processors become the paper and pencil of the information age. Spreadsheets replace the slide rule of engineers and the calculating machines of office workers. Data bases replace cabinets full of papers. Those unable to operate these new tools are handicapped in the modern world.

4. *Yet, technology provides no "magic bullet." Indeed, the introduction of technology on a large scale often creates new problems to be addressed.*

There is a price to be paid. The ticket for admission to information technology is expensive. In addition to resources, it requires concerted effort on the part of many actors in society. This is no minor challenge.

5. *The goal should be the "mindful introduction" of technology into*

education, not flooding the mind and the school system with everything that technology can offer.

The cemetery of failed experiments is large. Supply-driven initiatives, the results of enthusiastic salesmanship on the part of technology zealots, do not work. Not all things work in all contexts. Selectivity is essential. Understanding what the new media can offer in each case is vital. Successful experiments start with a well-identified need, for which new technologies may be the appropriate answer.

Most experiments to introduce information technology have taken place in mature and rich economies, where the resources are ample and the teachers well qualified. But the path for developing countries, which lack those resources, remains largely uncharted.

Developing countries should focus first on areas where technology has been clearly shown to be cost effective in education. Several countries have had ample experience with the use of interactive radio, with broadcast television and with satellites. Indeed, broadcast radio and television have respectable and predictable cost-effectiveness in many areas of basic education. They have been shown to be effective at early ages (e.g., "Sesame Street"). They tend to enhance equity, since they can reach a large pool of students and youth at modest per-participant costs. In several cases, these initiatives have been created and supported by the private sector, unburdening the State from their everyday operations and their costs. However, these solutions work best when integrated into national educational strategies.

There is no reason to underestimate the potential of computers. In fact, they have demonstrated a track record of success in industrial training applications, particularly in situations where the requisite feedback and evaluation is provided. Nevertheless, experience in the school context is more mixed. There are good examples of successful implementation, yet one cannot ignore the number of failures and near failures. Nor can we ignore the high costs involved, compared both to distance education and to conventional classroom delivery.

Networking technologies are newer and there is no established track record to guide us. They are expensive, requiring computers before the investments for connectivity are considered. Worse, their cost-effectiveness in improving education has not yet been established. However, they are believed to create new opportunities for creativity and learning. Countries which can afford the resources (Israel, Ireland, Singapore, Malaysia, Canada and the U.S.) are beginning to implement them. And judging from the use in private sector education institutions, computers and networking technologies are more than promising ideas.

THE PUBLIC POLICY DILEMMA

The decision to use distance education technology tends to be quite straightforward. With a large enough audience, the unit costs are known to be low, their effectiveness tends to be high and they tend to enhance equity (since they reach large clienteles that would not otherwise have access to education).

But computer and network technology are another matter. To start with, they are capacity enhancing, not cost saving. Hence, the chances of offering them to a broad share of the school population are still remote. For these reasons, without explicit planning, they may do little for equity. In addition, at least until now, they do not generate savings in other inputs so as to reduce the cost of investment. Therefore, technology introduction means additional societal resources going into education and benefiting a relatively narrow clientele.

Societies have to gauge the potential benefits of introducing computer and networking technologies to schools. Public authorities will need to decide whether and how to mobilize the substantial resources required for successful incorporation of these technologies into the pedagogical process.

THE STRATEGIES TO BRING NEW TECHNOLOGIES INTO SCHOOLS

Who decides to bring computers or Internet to schools? They can be "pushed" from outside, by central administrators, or they can be "pulled" by the initiative of schools themselves.

Observation of decentralized countries such as the United States shows many schools "pulling" technology into the pedagogic endeavor. These "pull" solutions are likely to be more successful and to generate lower costs, since only truly motivated schools will go to the trouble of procuring technology. Often, voluntary labor of parents is mobilized, equipment is donated by business, and charitable institutions contribute resources.

But these "pull" solutions exacerbate inequality because the schools which take such initiatives tend to be richer and have wealthier students and a more motivated and competent faculty.

European countries have tended to use "push" strategies. Such strategies are more demanding, as long-term commitments from public authorities are required. They also require system-wide rethinking of pedagogy and curriculum. In addition, experience shows that they are doomed to failure unless at least 30 percent of allocated budgets are used for training.

THE STAKES ARE HIGH

The following statements, taken from reports on the subject, indicate the urgency of the present situation:

"Countries which temporize, or favor half-hearted solutions, could, in less than a decade, face disastrous declines in investment and a squeeze on jobs." (European Union Commission Report)

Either the educational systems of Latin America "invest heavily in R&D and endure the 'information economy' metamorphosis, or they become unimportant and unexploitable." (Fernando Henrique Cardoso)

"The poor quality of the infrastructure in Latin America and the Caribbean is likely to result in a deterioration of the competitiveness and relative quality of life in the region, because other regions and countries are rapidly upgrading their infrastructure." (UNDP 1997)

Section 1

The Challenges of Bringing Technology to Education

A technological revolution in education is becoming possible, even though it has not yet happened.... Unless we learn to overcome the gap between the culture of technology and the culture of the school, we risk wasting this golden chance to improve education.

> What is good for the United States is not necessarily good for Latin America.... What is good for Latin America is what is affordable for the masses and what compensates for the chronic scarcity of quality teachers.
> (Claudio de Moura Castro)

I hope I have created a sense of urgency and a sense of enormous possibility. What is needed most is a sense of vision. And the private sector is a natural and willing partner in realizing that vision.
(W. Bowman Cutter)

Technology is not an educational activity; it is a tool—a means to an end. Technologies can be effective if they are designed and implemented deliberately to enhance students' engaged learning and collaboration. The key questions for education planners continue to be about how children grow and mature, what people need to know, how they construct and share that knowledge and how they interact with each other using such knowledge. (Wadi Haddad)

The only route to increasing the supply of education proportionate to the increasing demand is through the systematic and rational application of new information technologies to the process.
(Alexander Romiszowski)

Technology today offers many exciting alternative paths for improving education, but each of these alternatives is not equally good or appropriate for all countries.
(Claudio de Moura Castro)

Introdu

The technological revolution holds great promise for education. Technology in communication, image and data processing is evolving at lightning speed, while also becoming cheaper and more reliable. The consequences for education are enormous. Technology has gone from being a set of solutions in search of problems to increasingly offering precise and well-defined potential for education. A technological revolution in education is becoming possible, even though it has not yet happened.

Latin America lags behind other parts of the world in education. This has become a bottleneck given the new patterns of economic development taking over the globe. Technology seems to offer an opportunity to leapfrog the slow pace of development imposed by the traditional models of schooling. When the industrial countries implement new instruction technologies, they add that to an already mature system with the best of the conventional methods. In contrast, the greatest promise for Latin America and the Caribbean would be to have technology replace the more conventional means which poor countries cannot afford for the majority of the students.

While technology offers great potential, however, in most cases sociological and institutional barriers prevent this technological revolution from invading conventional schools. Some technologies remain stubbornly outside schools while they thrive in business environments and often in non-formal education. Unless we learn to overcome the gap between the culture of technology and the culture of the school, we risk wasting this golden chance to improve education.

There are economic and pedagogical reasons for introducing new technologies in education. First, it may be *cheaper to do it with technology*. As costs go down and the tools perform better, research shows more situations where technology is a better economic situation. Even though the opposite may be true for some uses (with technology resulting in higher costs), the potential to obtain more with fewer resources is a strong argument for using information technology in instruction. Furthermore, some of the new instruction technologies may be superior tools, compared to conventional teaching. Cognitive psychology and research suggest that higher levels of learning can be obtained in some cases.

Still, there is a culture shock when new technologies are brought to schools. There is resistance because it *disrupts conventional forms of organized teaching*. Traditional methods of organizing schools and teaching do not allow the most creative and productive deployment of information technologies. By the same token, conventional schools resist uses that disrupt their ingrained routines. In the most successful cases, it has been necessary to create new organizations and non-formal learning environments specially designed to deliver technologically intensive instruction.

In the first paper in this section, **"Education for All in the Age of Globalization: the Role of Information Technology,"** Wadi Haddad suggests that education must respond to the challenges of globalization and to the avalanche of new knowledge. Not only that, but it is no longer possible to offer a good education just for a few. A quality education for all is an imperative for progress. And to realize such an ambitious goal, technology may be one of the critical responses. The path to technology is not easy, however, requiring a long sequence of actions that would allow its introduction.

The second paper, **"Education in the Information Age: Promises and Frustrations"** by Claudio de Moura Castro, presents one of the core ideas which guided the organization of the Cartagena Seminar *Education in the Information Age*. The key issue is the significant difference between computers and the technologies used in distance education (e.g., TV, video, radio, correspondence and Internet). The latter tend to reach where conventional education does not go and operate at significantly lower costs. They avoid rejection by the educational establishment by creating and tailoring the institutions that deliver the instruction. Latin America excels in the use of these distance technologies, and is a world leader in the area. By contrast, computers tend to increase the cost of instruction, in order to offer an education which can enrich conventional learning methods. They also require the best possible teachers, which are scarce in the region. Furthermore, when they are deployed in existing academic schools, they face serious problems of rejection or partial and inadequate utilization.

Jeff Puryear discusses the economics of using new technologies in his paper **"The Economics of Educational Technology."** He shows that the technologies with a high fixed cost (the cost of producing the courseware and purchasing equipment) and low variable costs (by saving on teacher time) can lead to lower costs per student. However, this is only the case if the scale of utilization is sufficiently large to divide the fixed cost into a large number of students. The classical example is educational television and interactive radio, which can indeed be offered to millions of students at very modest costs. By contrast, when technology generates high variable costs, as is the case with computers in classrooms, the final result is higher costs, even though the superior results might justify them.

"The Half-life of Knowledge and Structural Reform" by Peter Knight discusses options in the organization of learning according to what he calls the "half-life" of knowledge. Skills which have a long half-life, such as those acquired in academic schools, are better left to public providers and public budgets. By contrast, those skills which are very specific or specialized and have a short half-life are better left to private operators, who can offer them on a commercial basis and recoup the costs—which are more modest and usually affordable by the users.

Alexander Romiszowski reviews the current state of technologies for human resource development in **"New Technologies for Human Resource Development."** He observes the changing nature of work, the need for a more creative and flexible work force, and the need for just-in-time training. Computer instruction and distance education become increasingly important in this new environment. However, there are many debates on the nature of this interaction. Computers and computer networks are becoming increasingly important in internal firm-based training as well as in more formal distance education. In the future, individuals will need to constantly update their skills. The formal residential university may well become outdated as networks increasingly carry the brunt of teaching in higher education both pre-and in-service.

In **"Instructional Technology—Then and Now,"** Laurence Wolff compares instructional technology in 1974 with the situation today. He finds that technology is now more flexible and interactive, there are many choices, and costs are much lower. However, many elements have not changed, the most important of which are the need to start with an educational problem rather than a particular technology and the need for a systems approach to integrate technology into the classroom.

The last paper in this section is based on a speech by W. Bowman Cutter on **"The View from the Private Sector: Needs and Opportunities."** Cutter emphasizes the political change toward open economies and the technological changes toward decreased communication and information processing costs. These changes are having global effects which require the public and private sectors to work together.

Education For All in the Age of Globalization
The Role of Information Technology

After decades of international studies and experiences, it is well recognized that education is crucial for economic development, human welfare, societal advancement and environmental protection. Based on this consensus, the World Conference on Education for All, held in Jomtien in 1990, called for meeting the basic learning needs for all children, youth and adults. These needs were to include "essential learning tools (such a literacy, oral expression, numeracy and problem solving) and the basic learning content (such as knowledge, skills, values and attitudes) required by human beings to be able to survive, to develop their full capacities, to live and work in dignity, to participate fully in development, to improve the quality of their lives, to make informed decisions, and to continue learning." Jomtien defined access to and equity of educational opportunities in terms of learning acquisition:

Wadi D. Haddad

Dr. Haddad is Special Adviser to the Director-General, UNESCO

Whether or not expanded educational opportunities will translate into meaningful development – for an individual or for society— depends ultimately on whether people actually learn as a result of those opportunities, i.e., whether they incorporate useful knowledge, reasoning ability, skills, and values.

EDUCATION FOR ALL IN THE AGE OF GLOBALIZATION

Since Jomtien, the world has experienced major developments:

- Changing patterns in trade and competition

- Drastic innovations in technology, telecommunications and informatics

- Fast exponential generation of knowledge and dramatic advancement in the dissemination of knowledge

These changes are producing a worldwide economy that is global, high speed, knowledge driven, disciplinarian and competitive. This requires a workplace characterized by agility, networking, teaming, productivity, quality and flexibility.

WHAT ARE THE IMPLICATIONS FOR EDUCATION FOR ALL?

1. *Placing education for all within a holistic structure.* Basic education vs. higher levels of education is an artificial or false dichotomy. The demands of a global economy leave countries with no choice but to invest in building the whole pyramid of knowledge and skills.

2. *Redefining education to mean maintenance of learning before, during, and after schooling,* and a curriculum that is elastic and flexible to cope with the new knowledge and economy.

3. *Reorienting education systems so that the skills of information assessment, sense making and knowledge construction become basic learning needs.* It is no longer enough to achieve mastery of content and skills. The need is for a different education that enhances the ability of the learners to access, assess, adopt and apply knowledge; to think independently, exercise appropriate judgment and collaborate with others to make sense of new situations.

4. *Ensuring time and space for reflective learning, creative expression and*

building of learning communities. The challenge is to keep learning in perspective as a process of making sense of information, understanding things in context and learning how to act and function effectively as a member of a community, or of several communities. Howard Gardner has helped identify the multiple intelligences with which people learn and express themselves. Gardner assigns particular importance to reflective intelligence, or meta-cognition. The core tasks of the learning support systems of the future include facilitating opportunities for reflective learning, creative expression and building of learning communities through sharing, dialogue and interactions with others trying to make sense of their environment and gain control over their lives.

These four implications pose a daunting challenge for the education strategist.

On the one hand:

● An avalanche of new knowledge

● Great uncertainties about the labor market

● New demands on education in uncharted territories

On the other hand:

● The need to address social concerns for equity and poverty alleviation

● Limited physical and human resources

● An ever-expanding base of education clientele.

Business as usual will not meet the challenge. Linear projections will not do. It is time for a radical rethinking of education.

Enter information technology

Compact discs and CD-ROMs, videodiscs, micro-computer-based laboratories, the Internet, virtual reality, local and wide area networks, instructional software, Macs, PCs, laptops, notebooks, educational television, voice mail, e-mail, satellite communication, VCRs, Cable TV, interactive radio... the list of "hot" technologies available for education goes on and on. Can these technologies help the education strategist face the challenge of an education for all in an age of globalization? Educators have at many times before been told that certain technologies would remake their world—from movable type to filmstrips to radio to television. Is it any different this time? Two boundary conditions:

1. Technology is not an educational activity; it is a tool—a means to an end. Technologies can be effective if they are designed and implemented deliberately to enhance students' engaged learning and collaboration. The key questions for education planners continue to be about how children grow and mature, what people need to know, how they construct and share that knowledge and how they interact with each other using such knowledge.

The new findings from brain science and genetics about how people learn can change our thinking about how to use technology for effective learning. It can be a breakthrough. In neuroscience, new brain scans will take almost instantaneous pictures of brain activity. The MRI will safely image the brains of learners and show step-by step how the most complicated information-processing device in the world becomes wired.

2. There is a basic difference between using technology to make the present model of education more efficient, more equitable and cheaper, on the one hand, and injecting technology into the entire education system to realize structural rethinking and re-engineering on the other. It is a difference between a marginal addition and a radical systemic change. It is in the second scenario that technology can provide the greatest impact. This opportunity was clearly articulated by Louis V. Gerstner, Jr., Chairman and CEO of IBM, in a 1995 speech to the U.S. National Governors' Association:

> Information technology is the fundamental underpinning of the science of structural re-engineering. It is the force that revolutionizes business, streamlines government and enables instant communications and the exchange of information among people and institutions around the world. But information technology has not made even its barest appearance in most public schools.... Before we can get the education revolution rolling, we need to recognize that our public schools are low-tech

institutions in a high-tech society. The same changes that have brought cataclysmic change to every face of business can improve the way we teach students and teachers. And it can also improve the efficiency and effectiveness of how we run our schools.

ROLE OF INFORMATION TECHNOLOGY

Within these two boundary conditions of learning-oriented technology and educational structural re-engineering, information technology can have a monumental impact in four areas:

1. Improvement of learning and instructions

Technology can be very powerful as an instructional tool for basic skills. It is infinitely patient with drill-and-practice. It can store and retrieve immense databanks of facts, sample problems, exercises and other curriculum resources. These are the areas in which the information management technologies are most valuable—storing, processing and retrieving information, with the possibilities of endlessly going over the same material in a variety of forms and media, layering in additional information and nuances of understanding while re-enforcing the learning objectives. Networking is useful for such applications, but is not essential—most of what is needed can be accomplished with local area networks at the level of the school or classroom and most information can be accessed and managed at least as effectively using floppy disks, CD-ROMs, video and other media. In such applications, the quality of the software and its alignment with the intended curriculum is extremely important.

It is important to note that the above characteristics also make it possible to design applications for almost any learning need, including children with physical limitations, isolated children or learners whose education was disrupted, individuals with specific delays or learning problems. Arguably, as countries approach universal schooling, the ability of technology to help address special learning needs with cost-effective approaches may be one of its most valued characteristics.

Technology also can be powerful in driving new approaches to learning that involve more student interaction, more connections among schools, more collaboration among teachers and students, more involvement of teachers as facilitators and more emphasis on the skills of information seeking and assessment, exploration of open questions, problem-solving, critical thinking, design and construction of new knowledge and understandings. A key understanding is that these new approaches are quite different, with different objectives. A 10-year study supported by Apple Computer concluded that students in technology-rich learning environments not only scored well on standardized tests but also developed a variety of competencies not usually measured—abilities to explore and represent information dynamically and in many forms; problem-solving; social awareness and confidence; communications skills; independent learning skills; and self-knowledge about areas of expertise.

In developing public policy and strategies for making more effective use of these technologies, it is important to develop broad understanding of these objectives and to expect outcomes. It is in these areas that the networking, connectivity and interactivity characteristics of the information technologies become somewhat more important. In such applications, the ease of communication (including e-mail) and the ability of learners to form user groups and find collaborators and to search for other information sources may be important characteristics.

2. Improvement of policy planning, design and data management

Education policy development is an intricate process that requires reliable and timely data that are policy-oriented and user-friendly. Here information can be valuable in storing and analyzing data on education indicators, student assessment, physical and human educational infrastructure, cost and finance. The technology can help not only in diagnosis but, more importantly, it can assist in constructing scenarios around different intended policy options to determine requirements and consequences. Each scenario can then be systematically analyzed and evaluated, not only in terms of its educational desirability but also in terms of financial affordability, feasibility and sustainability over a sufficient period of time to show results.

3. Support of educational personnel

Technology allows teachers to overcome the isolation they experience in their schools and provides them with continuous professional development. For example videodiscs, CD-ROMs and distance learning technologies can be used to deliver staff development courses led by top-of-the-line experts. Connected to an information infrastructure, teachers can communicate with other teachers and professionals and can access data banks, libraries and other vast stores of information. As technology in the school allows teachers to perform traditional task with a speed and quality that were unattainable before, it will permit better use of their time not only to teach differently but also to develop professionally.

4. Improvement of school management

The same elements of computing and telecommunications equipment and service that made businesses more efficient and cost-effective can be applied to schools and school systems to enable principals and superintendents to streamline operations, monitor performance and improve utilization of physical and human resources. Technology also has the potential to support the management of complex, standards-related instructional processes in ways that have previously been achieved by only the most advanced schools and skilled teachers. It can also promote communication among schools, parents, central decision-makers and businesses, fostering greater accountability, public support and connectivity with the marketplace.

HOW CAN THIS HAPPEN?

Many countries across the world are responding to the demands of the information age and already making substantial investments in technology for education. Meeting the challenges listed above requires deliberate action on four fronts:

1. A reorientation of the curriculum and learning environment to allow for the best use of information technology.

2. An accelerated investment in information infrastructure, including computers, connectivity, electricity and personnel. The costs are modest in the context of overall budget, but they still require significant and potentially painful budgetary restructuring in the short term. In the long term it is predicted that within the next 25 years the power of microelectronics will increase a million-fold and their cost will drop dramatically. Also, the cost of public data communications will drop one hundred-fold. The Internet will surpass our present-day

expectations and will become a cheap household item.

3. A deliberate program of professional orientation and training so that teachers and administrators can learn both how to use the technology and how to integrate it into this curriculum.

4. Software development. Despite the growth of education software availability, software companies continue to avoid investing in the field. They argue that the national school market is too small to generate a profit. Here, we hope that countries will collaborate to produce curriculum-related software that can be used world-wide. Applying the economies of scales, these investments can be very cost-effective. UNESCO, with the support of Member States, foundations and the private sector, can take the initiative in leading this effort.

I conclude with two quotations:

> *Technology is important to all the schools across the country, because without technology we will be second all the time. We don't want to be second.*
>
> —*Student, U.S.A.*

> *Technology, in and of itself, is not a magic wand. Technology is not going to fix the problems associated with schooling. But at the same time, the problems that plague our educational system are not going to be remedied without the presence of technology.*
>
> —*Researcher*

Education in the Information Age
Promises and Frustrations

Claudio de Moura Castro

Computers have been visiting schools for a quarter of a century. Television was first used for education in the fifties, soon after it was created. Why do we still call them "new instructional technologies"? Both technologies were announced as a revolution. Has it taken place? Has education been shaken as a result of their existence? How is Latin America affected by all this?

This paper explores the successes and failures of information technologies in education. It points to their great potential: the tangible dream of using them to bring serious education to a vast number of people. But it also points to the difficulties of fulfilling this dream, due to modes of utilization that fail to capture the potential offered by the vast array of technological innovations in existence.

The key argument of the paper can be summarized as follows. Information technology can be used to compensate for what conventional systems cannot afford to offer. If this is done, the reach of serious education can be extended to reach populations who otherwise would have much poorer-quality instruction or none at all. Alternatively, information technology can be used in conjunction with factors which are scarce and expensive, such as highly trained and motivated teachers. This combination might lead to levels of learning which would not be possible without it; but it will reach only as far as these other factors do—namely, not very far in the case of Latin America.

Used in classrooms in a constructivist approach, computers have tremendous potential to develop students' higher-order cognitive skills. (The premise of constructivism is that knowledge is constructed by the learner rather than imparted by the teacher. Its tools are those that extend students' capacities to explore and experiment.) However, computers require exactly the kind of teachers which are scarce everywhere in the world. They also require considerable capital outlays and infrastructure. By contrast, high-quality broadcast television programs benefit from pre-existing investment in hardware, economize on high quality teachers by having them serve as support to less than superbly trained monitors, and have strong economies of scale. Whether the levels of learning are comparable to those from conventional modes of delivery is an open question. But what TV programs do is to allow the skills and imagination of the best teachers available to reach a clientele that otherwise could never dream of access to that level of education.

If this reasoning is correct, the policy implications are very significant. Poorer countries should focus their efforts less on uses of technology which try to reach beyond what is possible with good quality conventional education. Instead, they should focus on reaching the poor through cost-effective technology that compensates for the limitations of conventional education.

THE PATH FROM TECHNOLOGY TO EDUCATION

All major developments in the transmission of images and in the development of computers took place in the industrialized countries. The same, of course, is true for the subsequent technologies such as videotape, CD-ROMs, interactive TV and the Internet. Therefore, it should be no surprise that the first educational uses of these technologies took place in the industrialized countries, and in particular in the United States. From the first uses of broadcast TV in Michigan during the 1950s to the early experiments in using mainframe computers in tutorial programs such as Plato, most seminal innovations took place in the U.S. However, European countries in the last several years have taken computer use seriously, and their performance in this area in some ways may be more successful than that of the Americans.

When these developments took place in the U.S. and Europe, these countries had mature and high-performing systems of education compared to Third World countries. Virtually all children were in school and stayed there as long as prescribed by law. They also had access to properly qualified teachers and could afford high education costs by the standards of non-industrialized countries.

The idea of using a computer instead of a teacher may have created a great scare in the teaching profession, but it was short-lived and never pursued with much zeal. The idea of using television instead of schools or teachers never went very far, either, except in the case of isolated communities or with children too young to go to school (e.g., "Sesame Street").

The first uses of both computers and TV tended to mimic teachers. The initial batch of tutorial software and the more widespread use of "drill and practice" programs used machines to repeat what teachers do in conventional classrooms. They taught simple skills or trained students in them, such as spelling and multiplication tables. Educational TV had teachers in front of the camera teaching the same classes they would in more conventional classroom situations – the "talking head" version of educational TV.

But soon computers were being upgraded to more imaginative uses. The turtle which moved around on the screen was seen as a means to teach programming algorithms. LOGO became a landmark in the use of computers to develop higher-order learning. Simulations and animations offer endless potential to make students understand theoretical principles. From graphic models of the solar system to a vast range of chapters in physics or inference statistics or the Electronic Workbench, a computer can show what scientific abstractions are about.

The fuzzy borders of educational software and "edutainment" opened another fruitful path to understanding the world and playing at the same time. Oregon Trail and Carmen San Diego were incredibly successful pieces of software mixing games and school subjects. (Teachers never really liked the game part—but that is something else.) There are hundreds in the same spirit on the market.

Word processors offered a new path to writing. "Spell-checkers" changed the rules in the art of spelling words. None of this was planned, yet word processors have become one of the most robust uses of computers in education.

Following the approach recently christened as constructivism, computers are being proposed as tools to explore the world. This may be via computers equipped with sensors as data gathering devices, or via data bases. Whatever the tool, students are urged to research, explore and express themselves in ways which are not possible, practical or powerful with more conventional means.

The emergence of the Internet brought another wave of innovations and enthusiasm for the use of computers. From early experiments in connecting schools to Dow Jones data bases to the cacophony of present day web sites, the possibilities are mind-boggling.

At the same time, the dissemination of the VHS video system made it possible to bring a wealth of images to students. From watching surgery with better visibility than in the operating room to student-produced videos, this proved to be a highly powerful tool. Beyond that, the recording of conventional classes allows students to stop and repeat, improving learning and retention. In a classical experiment, Hewlett Packard engineers studied by watching a videotape of a Stanford electrical engineering graduate program. Achievement tests showed that the Hewlett Packard engineers performed better than the Stanford students, giving increased respectability to the distance education alternatives.

A new line of programs identified with the BBC, the Discovery Channel and The Learning Channel again blurred the line between entertainment, culture and education. Along yet another path, corporations have noticed the potential of these media and adopted them as a routine feature of their training programs. Even more extensive uses of instructional technology are found in the armed forces of industrial countries.

THE ECONOMICS OF TEACHING WITH MACHINES

In conventional teaching, the time of teachers remains the most important element of the costs. In most cases, it accounts for more than half of total costs. In contrast, the fixed costs tend to be modest: the use of the building and equipment and the relatively rudimentary preparation of teaching materials. Under those conditions, there are no significant returns to scale. As long as there are enough students to fill one class, it matters little whether they number a dozen or a million.

Exactly the opposite is true with technology-intensive teaching. The fixed costs predominate and the variable costs are much lower. First of all, the machines must be purchased. Computers cost at least three thousand dollars if peripherals, rewiring and other technical costs are included. TV sets and VCRs and parabolic antennas cost less than that, but still are far more expensive than any other piece of equipment used in traditional classrooms. When we consider the infrastructure necessary for broadcast transmissions of TV signals, the numbers are not at all modest. Satellite reception requires additional equipment that remains expensive despite price drops. By the same token, software for computers and teaching materials for TV programs are very expensive when they are good.

Variable costs, however, tend to be quite modest with technology-intensive teaching. The main component is instructors or other forms of labor. The variable costs relate to the conventional end of new instructions—namely, the teachers and aides who use them.

The implications of this distribution of costs could not be clearer. The use of new technologies is associated with powerful economies of scale. As noted, under conventional teacher-intensive technologies per capita costs tend to remain the same or almost the same whether there are one hundred or one million students. In contrast, with new technologies, cost depends on how many share the fixed costs of preparation and installation of equipment. A TV program such as Telecurso 2000, which cost close to 50 million dollars to develop, will have a cost per student of five thousand dollars if 1000 students attend and ten dollars if 5 million students attend. The latter figure is not an unreasonable prediction for this program during its lifetime. Educational software which typically may cost $300,000 to produce is usually sold at twenty or thirty dollars, due to the huge scale of sales.

Therefore, it is the expected scale of utilization which should determine the mode of instruction. With few students, one hires a teacher; with thousands of students, technology-intensive alternatives may be less expensive. It is assumed that for every hour of classroom contact, a teacher has to invest another hour of preparation. For every hour of class, it takes five hours to prepare written materials. But every hour of instruction using an interactive CD Rom requires at least 300 hours of preparation. Hence, in order to justify the use of more complex instructional technologies, it is necessary to have a much broader clientele.

These considerations are important because Latin American countries cannot afford to ignore the costs of education in its different modalities. Even our most affluent countries have difficulty making ends meet. Hence, it should be no surprise that they cannot afford the same technologies being used in the industrialized nations. In many cases, the alternatives are either to have expensive technologies for a privileged few, or to have more economical alternatives for a larger share of the school-aged population.

Television and other forms of distance education cost less than computers in schools. As noted, a computer costs at least three thousand dollars. Assuming a useful life of five years and another three hundred dollars of maintenance per year, we have six hundred dollars per computer per year. Taking the rate of 1 computer to every ten students, this amounts to $60 per year. Assuming an average cost of $300 per student for basic education, using computers will increase educational expenditures by 20 percent. This is not a politically feasible increase in educational budgets.

THE THEORY AND THE THEORY OF THE PRACTICE IN USING TECHNOLOGY

There have been a dizzying number of experiments, many of them conducted by teams with a strong scientific background and the capacity and inclination to conduct controlled experiments and rigorous evaluation studies.

Many of those studies indicate that new instructional technologies may bring strong and positive improvements in learning. Indeed, rigorous studies show that most major forms of computer utilization in classrooms have a positive impact on learning. Drill and practice, tutorial programs, word processors, IBM's Writing to Read—there is no dearth of serious and credible studies showing how under well-controlled conditions it is possible to obtain gains in learning with the use of computers. Another group of studies also shows distance education to be effective. In fact, correspondence education is at least one century old, and study after study shows positive results.

Scaling up is another matter, however. Cognitive theory says that such-and-such technology works fine in improving learning, implying that all it takes to achieve the educational revolution is to scale it up. But the theory of the practice is another matter, as scaling up is much harder than expected. It may indeed be true that if applied to everybody, the effects would amount to a small educational revolution. The problem is that what works under a controlled and protected atmosphere may fail when scaled up.

Educational experiments create a total environment which is designed to shelter the project. In scaling up, however, the innovation has to face a real world that is far less hospitable. Schools are conservative organizations and their incentive structures are very hard to change. Very often, they welcome small experiments which do not threaten conventional operations. But scaling up affects the rules of the game and may conflict with school values, practices and incentives. Hence, it is resisted, boycotted, sabotaged or discretely abandoned. As a result, the scaled-up program does not look at all like the small experiment which seemed so promising. More often, the scaling up does not even take place, due to passive or active resistance.

A consequence of the theory of the practice is that costs are not as low as expected, because of waste, breakdowns, under-utilization and misuse. Therefore, not only are the results a pale image of what the pilot projects promised, but the costs per students tend to be much higher.

The results of this lack of effectiveness of scaled-up activities and the cost overruns are far more serious for Latin American countries, because they are less capable of affording such waste. In rich countries, the costs of technology are a much smaller fraction of education costs. Notice that a computer in an American school costs, at most, just half of the student/year cost while in Latin America it costs ten times more than to keep one student in school during the same period. The Clinton proposal to wire all schools to the Internet and equip them with more and better computers increases total costs of K12 education by no more than one or two percentage points during one year.

"WHAT IS GOOD FOR THE UNITED STATES..."?

It was once said that what was good for the United States was also good for Latin America. Whether this is true in particular situations is a moot point. But in the case of instructional technologies, this is certainly not the case. The United States, like other rich countries, can afford most if not all of these technologies, even if they do not work too well.

It stands to reason that they choose and scale up the technologies which respond to their needs. And their needs are the needs of countries which have already put into their schools just about everything that has been dreamed up by educators and administrators.

Not only is universal education provided through secondary school, but the availability of post-secondary education allows motivated students to continue. With the exception of a few remote regions, there are as many properly trained and certified teachers as there are subjects being offered.

Therefore, instructional technologies are used to take the additional step, to improve learning beyond the levels previously reached—levels already vastly superior to those reached by Latin America. In other words, they are used not to save resources or to reach a broader clientele but to raise the quality of education even further.

In Latin America, the problem with the use of instructional technology is that too often its champions studied in the United States or Europe, following the meandering intellectual fashions of these regions. No matter how poor the country, very often those struggling to introduce instructional technology are closely following the latest paper published in computer journals.

When the latest fashion meant drill and practice programs for computers, this was a relatively easy technology to apply. However, the state of the art has evolved from that to LOGO, to simulations, to the introduction of computers in regular disciplines, to the Internet and to the World Wide Web.

Rich schools in poor countries have done quite well in following the examples of rich countries. In fact, most of the positive experience using computers in schools takes place in private schools catering to the higher layers of society. There is nothing intrinsically wrong with this. In fact, private schools have become the experimental grounds for the best the hemisphere has to offer in the use of computers in schools. This pool of experienced teachers will eventually have spillovers for the public system.

Even so, these uses commit a capital sin for poor countries. *They require exactly the factors which are particularly scarce in poor countries— namely, resources and well-trained teachers.* If poor countries had a vast supply of the teachers needed for LOGO or constructivist approaches to computer utilization, they would not have the miserable education they do. By the same token, with about ten (bad quality) telephone lines to each hundred inhabitants, the Internet is doomed to remain an elitist resource, available only to a small number of students. No less important, these remain expensive technologies for Latin America, even with falling costs over the last several decades.

The bottom line, therefore, is obvious enough. What is good for the United States is not necessarily good for Latin America. Latin America should resist the temptation to mimic the use of instructional technologies of the Northern countries, because it is not compatible with its present factor endowments. We have neither the abundant financial resources nor the supply of well-trained teachers necessary to scale up even the most creative use of computers in the classroom.

Surely, the above statement is not meant to deny the right to pursue state-of-the-art technology. In fact, as technologies evolve and costs go down, countries are well-advised to hone their skills in the use of these technologies, no matter how arcane or expensive they may be at present. But we should make a strong distinction between a policy of encouraging small experiments in all directions and the thrust of a global policy to use new instructional technologies in our countries. This general principle is not restricted to computers in education; there are several other technologies, such as interactive television, which remain too expensive to reach large numbers of students. These run the risk of being too expensive to be scaled up without resulting in frightening costs per student when operated at the small scales permitted by the narrow budgets available.

WHAT IS GOOD FOR LATIN AMERICA

What is good for Latin America is what is affordable for the masses and what compensates for the chronic scarcity of quality teachers. Fortunately, the quest for "teacher-proof teaching methods" is *passé* and the fear that computers will create mass unemployment of teachers has abated. Certainly this paper is not proposing a reinstatement of those goals.

What we are proposing is that instructional technologies should compensate for the shortcomings of existing teachers or for their complete absence in very poor regions. Just as rich countries have used technology to respond to their needs, we are suggesting that in Latin America technology should respond to our needs.

In the case of computers in schools, software must be easy to use and non-threatening to the teachers. Unavoidably, this means that the most interesting and enriching uses of computers will have to wait. Can we use the expression "appropriate technology" without insulting everybody?

Another suggested line is to privilege those institutions which have less fear of computers, such as technical and vocational schools or educational institutions. An alternate approach is to favor those created expressly to use new technologies—a trend that began with the creation of the United Kingdom's Open University in response to the refusal of the traditional British universities to engage in distance education. It has been noted again and again that K-12 schools are the ones which most resist the use of technologies, making waste higher and results less impressive.

Probably the starkest contrast is between the modest, or in some cases outright disappointing, results of computers in academic schools and the impressive use of broadcast TV for education. While Latin America, at best, plays second fiddle in the area of computers in schools, the experiments in using television for mass education are nothing short of spectacular and as good as anything done anywhere else in the world.

Rich countries have used television in education in very modest ways. The BBC may be an illustrious exception. Programs for pre-schoolers, such as "Sesame Street" and others associated with PBS, cater to populations not served by regular schools and have also fared quite well. But by and large, educational TV in rich countries does not amount to very much. All one needs to do to verify this proposition is to surf the cable channels and contrast the quality, tempo, color, and wealth of images on commercial networks with the "talking heads" lecturing on standard school subjects on the local educational TV channels.

By contrast, Mexico has been operating its Telesecundária for many years, with millions of students having gone through its courses. For these students, Telesecundária was not just a good option but the only way to attend secondary school. Also in Mexico are the impressive achievements of the Tecnologico de Monterrey with its technical courses beamed to students in many states and now reaching several other countries with its technical and management courses.

Brazil, a country of modest achievements in education, has become a leader in the area of distance education, bringing forth many interesting innovations. From the 1960s on, two states (Maranhão and Ceará) have been operating secondary schools by TV, very much along the lines of Mexico. This has been an early and respectable if not very creative use of TV.

Far more impressive have been the achievements of Globo network. Recently it retired the old Telecurso, just short of its twentieth anniversary. While no reliable attendance statistics are available, it is safe to say that it has been watched or carefully followed by many millions of poor Brazilians. This program was replaced by the new Telecurso 2000, which also offers a GED-type program for young adults, with separate primary and secondary programs.

One interesting feature of this program is that it does not use the traditional classroom metaphor. All the classes take place in factories, offices, tourism agencies (for English language), newspaper stands and so on. Faithful to the principles of contextualization of teaching, all materials are presented by means of concrete life situations. Young adults learn by watching scenes which are close to their worlds, rather than the stale classroom with a teacher and students. In fact, the program uses professional actors for all scenes except for some quick interviews with well-known professors.

Another interesting innovation is the concept of redundancy on the delivery of the programs. They are broadcast between six and seven in the morning, when workers are often watching television while they get ready to leave home. Educational TV stations rebroadcast the programs in the afternoon or evening. Many users videotape the program in order to view them at a more convenient time. In addition, the tapes are sold to interested parties at very modest prices. The written materials that follow the course are sold in newsstands.

Curiously, this is a strictly private initiative. It is funded by the Federation of Industries of São Paulo, which wanted a program to allow enterprises to train their workers. By the end of 1997, the number of students participating in organized reception in specially equipped classrooms with instructors was expected to approach half a million. The number of people watching the programs in the morning for a combination of learning and entertainment already reaches 1.4 million in the city of São Paulo alone.

Perhaps as noteworthy as the previous points is the fact that the quality of the programs equals that of the best commercial TV. In that sense, these are programs which boast the same quality of acting, sets, scripts and tempo as high-quality commercial TV.

Along the same lines, TV also offers privately-funded programs of agricultural extension and small business development. The audience for these programs is extraordinarily high, reaching millions. Recently, the Federation of Transports, representing private business in the area, rented satellite time and started offering 10 hours per day of training in transport-related trades. There are already 1,200 classrooms spread around the country, mostly in transportation firms, with enrollment that reaches 300,000.

What all these experiments have in common is that they reach the masses, which the conventional educational systems cannot always do. They also compensate for the inadequate preparation of teachers. Telecurso 2000 has classrooms with learning facilitators helping the students. But if these instructors were to teach the students, they could never deliver anything comparable to what can be done with professional actors reading scripts prepared by the best teachers in the country, in programs directed by professional TV people. Last but not least, these programs have low costs per student. Any cost divided into millions of students becomes inexpensive.

SOME LESSONS

To conclude, what this paper is saying is that technology today offers many exciting alternative paths for improving education, but each of these alternatives is not equally good or appropriate for all countries. Rich countries have used technology to make their good education even better. If Latin American countries were to follow the same path, they would be choosing alternatives which, in addition to being very expensive, require high-quality teachers who are not available and cannot be made available. These experiments are therefore doomed to remain enclaves, catering to local elites but incapable of being scaled up to reach the number of people who are in dire need of better instruction.

Instead, then, Latin America needs to focus on those technologies which compensate for the factors which are lacking—namely, well-trained teachers and the resources to pay for expensive equipment. Latin American countries should concentrate on those technological alternatives which, at low cost, bring to students the imagination and creativity of a few excellent teachers.

While the use of computers in classrooms is not to be denigrated, a much greater potential can be found in distance education. The fact of the matter is that despite considerable efforts to bring computers to academic classrooms, Latin America remains a marginal player in this area. This contrasts to the superlative and world-class performance of mass education programs using broadcast TV and video.

The Economics of Educational Technology

Jeffrey M. Puryear

Someone observed recently that the most important innovation in educational technology in Latin America over the past century or more has been blackboards and chalk. While that may sound like a trivial comment, in fact it is probably true, and understanding why it is true may help us think more clearly about the many new educational technologies being discussed in this book.

This paper looks at educational technology principally in economic terms and lays out the economic questions that should be asked about specific technologies. My goal is to identify the right questions, and then to say as much as possible about what the answers to those questions might be.

First, it is important to note that "educational technology" is a fairly broad term. Most experts include at least the following: print (chiefly textbooks but other printed materials as well), audio cassettes, programmed learning, radio, broadcast television, and personal computers. Peer tutoring programs are sometimes included. Even relatively low-tech approaches, such as slide projectors (or blackboards and

Mr. Puryear works with Inter-American Dialogue.

chalk), merit attention as promising technologies, particularly when resources are tight—which is usually the case in most of Latin America.

So, let us look for a moment at blackboards and chalk. What are their essential characteristics? They are cheap, readily available, portable, require nothing from the surrounding environment to function, need almost no maintenance, and can be mastered by anyone who possesses basic literacy. And they are effective in helping children learn at all educational levels—primary, secondary, and post-secondary.

That's pretty good. These are the qualities we might expect the ideal educational technology to have.

Blackboards and chalk in fact constitute a kind of benchmark. They help us see what questions to ask when assessing educational technologies. And it seems fair to ask how many of those new technologies possess all—or even a few—of the qualities possessed by blackboards and chalk.

Now if you look carefully at blackboards and chalk, it quickly becomes clear that their qualities can be divided into two categories: costs and effectiveness. Furthermore, it is clear that both costs and effectiveness are influenced significantly by something else that is independent of blackboards and chalk: the conditions in which they are expected to operate. So that suggests that in assessing educational technologies, there are at least three kinds of issues to look at: costs, effectiveness, and surrounding conditions. Only when we look at all three can we determine whether a given technology is suitable.

Let's look briefly at each of them.

COSTS

Technologies have at least two kinds of costs: fixed costs and variable costs. In this context, fixed costs are what it costs to put in place the necessary infrastructure and software for making the technology available. It is the up-front investment. In the case of textbooks, for example, it is usually just the cost of writing the books. In the case of television, it is the cost of establishing a broadcasting capacity and of producing the programs. In the case of computers, it is mostly the cost of writing appropriate programs. Fixed costs may also include the cost of setting up a central managerial and training system that is necessary to produce, distribute, implement, and maintain the technology.

Not surprisingly, fixed costs are different for different kinds of technology. The fixed costs of textbooks and other printed materials are fairly low, consisting mainly of payments to authors to write the books and materials. The fixed costs of radio and television are much higher, and consist of payments to produce and broadcast programs. Television costs considerably more to produce than radio—one estimate suggests 25 times more.

But fixed costs have an important quality: they are spread out over all the students served. We need to remember that the fixed cost per student for some educational technologies, such as radio and television, drops rapidly as more students are served, because of economies of scale. The fixed cost of an educational TV program that serves just 1000 students would be about the same as the fixed cost of a program that serves 100,000, or 1,000,000. You need the same up-front investment in producing programs. But the fixed cost per student drops rapidly when you can divide that cost by 100,000 students, or by a million, rather than by 1000. By contrast, approaches that have low fixed costs, such as conventional teaching—which relies exclusively on the time of teachers—offer no significant economies of scale.

Variable costs are what it costs to add students to the system after it has been set up. It is the cost of serving an additional student. For textbooks it is the cost of producing and distributing each additional book, and for computers it is the cost of providing and maintaining each additional computer and its programs, plus the additional cost of providing electricity and perhaps telephone service. Training teachers to use the new technology is also principally a variable cost; you must train additional teachers every time you introduce the technology to another classroom.

Variable costs also are different for different technologies. The variable cost of textbooks is low, particularly if the books are reused by each cohort of students. The variable cost of radio is also low, since radios are already widely available and can run on batteries if necessary. The variable cost of educational television is higher, perhaps 10 times as high as radio, since televisions cost more to purchase, require an electrical hook-up, and need more maintenance. The variable cost of computers is even higher—perhaps 100 times as expensive as radio—because of purchase and maintenance costs, and perhaps the cost of teacher training. Access to the Internet also requires a telephone line. Computer costs are, of course, a moving target and have dropped significantly during the past few years. But they remain high compared to traditional levels of per-student spending in Latin

America. The variable cost of conventional teaching is also fairly high, since you must pay an additional salary for every 30 or so students.

Another important aspect of technology costs is the way they fit into the educational system. Technologies designed to substitute for personal classroom teaching—many of the distance education programs, for example—have a built-in cost advantage: they make unnecessary many of the personnel costs of conventional schools. This is particularly the case for students who are in remote areas or highly dispersed geographically. Research suggests that distance education programs for training teachers, for example, can be developed at a cost of between one-third and two-thirds the cost of conventional programs.

By contrast, educational technology that requires significant supervised classroom teaching, or that is designed to complement the traditional activities of a teacher, is less likely to reduce costs. These programs usually incur both the costs of conventional schooling and the costs of the new technology. Some of them may also bring "hidden" costs by requiring new curricula, new roles for teachers, and a new managerial system. Governments might still choose such programs, of course, but they should do so because the learning increment is worth the additional cost, and not because they expect costs to be lower.

What does all of this tell us? First, that providers need to calculate both fixed and variable costs when assessing technology programs, and need to consider how many students they expect to serve.

Second, that technologies with high fixed costs and low variable costs—such as television and radio—can be quite inexpensive, if they serve large numbers of students. They yield greater economies of scale.

Third, that technologies with high variable costs, and that work in conjunction with conventional teaching—such as personal computers—are unlikely to bring any cost advantage. Indeed, they may be quite expensive.

Fourth, that technologies which replace conventional teaching, rather than complement it, are likely to have a cost advantage. Such technologies may allow setting up new programs that are cheaper per student than are traditional approaches. For this reason, the most successful applications of educational technology in developing countries have been in distance education programs, which provide services that conventional approaches cannot afford to provide.

And fifth, that technologies which are relatively self-contained, and require only minimal pedagogical input and managerial support at the local level may have a cost advantage. Again, radio and television stand out in this category. Some forms of programmed learning may also fall into this category.

EFFECTIVENESS

The next issue in assessing educational technology is effectiveness. Here the story is relatively simple. All our research and experience tell us that under the right circumstances and with sufficient resources, nearly any of the new educational technologies can be effective in improving learning.

Studies also suggest that technology does not have to be implemented large-scale in order to be successful and sustainable. Often, technology that fulfills a specific, narrowly defined purpose in the classroom and complements other educational goals has a greater chance of being effective. Clearly, effectiveness does not require that large quantities of technology be added across the entire educational system.

Interestingly enough, research fails to support the idea that more expensive or more complex technologies produce better educational outcomes. It appears that motivated students can learn from any medium that is competently used. To be sure, we have little research to date on the learning outcomes of computer and multimedia approaches; perhaps future research will yield different conclusions. But it is also true that relatively simple new technologies, such as electronic mail and off-the-shelf computer software, appear to give good results. Thus far, then, the idea that complicated, high-tech approaches are more effective than simple, low-tech ones has not been demonstrated.

The question therefore is not really whether technology is effective. It usually can be. Rather the question is, what does it take to make technology effective, and how much does that cost? In economic terms, we're talking about cost-effectiveness. We need to know whether the cost of successfully incorporating technology is a good investment.

Here, research is fairly limited, but it does suggest that some approaches are better than others. For example, distance education programs have often proven cost-effective, in part because they operate separately from, and in place of, conventional teaching. Interactive radio instruction has also been shown to be more cost-effective than textbooks under some circumstances.

Generally, however, research suggests that technology has a greater potential for improving effectiveness or expanding access than it does for reducing unit costs. So when we think about cost-effectiveness, we will more often need to decide that we are willing to pay more money to get more learning.

SURROUNDING CONDITIONS

The final issue is the surrounding conditions, which we will look at here principally in economic terms.

Claudio de Moura Castro noted in the previous paper that although many educational technologies have demonstrated their effectiveness, they have not been as widely adopted as predicted back in the 1960s and 1970s. Why not?

The reason for this appears to be that the conditions necessary for educational technology to be successful are often not present. These technologies need some combination of factors from their surrounding context—proper conditions—for success.

Economists call this combination of factors a production function. It specifies what output can be expected from any particular combination of inputs. The idea is to maximize output (in this case, learning) from the inputs you have available, and to be sure that the right mix of inputs is on hand so that each can do its job. When educational technology is adopted, then, the key questions are what combination of factors or conditions is necessary to make it work, and whether it is possible bring that combination together.

Some technologies, for example, require talented and highly motivated teachers in order to work. These may be scarce, particularly in public schools. Or they may require reliable electrical and telephone connections—often unavailable in rural areas. Or they may require sophisticated management and training systems that are beyond the capacity of some governments. They may require altering the traditional roles of teachers, which teachers may fiercely resist. Or they may require that ministry of education officials cede power and staff to new institutions, something government bureaucracies hate to do. They may simply cost more than governments are willing to pay, leading to underfunding.

Research suggests that the biggest obstacle to successfully adopting educational technology is establishing the political and institutional framework necessary to sustain the innovation. One of the most famous examples is the instructional television program in El Salvador, which reached nearly a quarter of a million students at its peak, and appeared to have been relatively effective, but which succumbed to political problems.

Several successes, most notably the Telesecundária program in Mexico and the instructional radio program in the Dominican Republic, owe their success to their ability to bring together the necessary set of conditions. Distance education programs have had their greatest success when carried out in higher education, where students are older and do not need the discipline, supervision, and motivation that younger students need. Also, higher education is one area where a good deal of unsatisfied demand for education exists, making it easier for distance learning programs to compete with conventional schools. The success of open universities in several countries, including Colombia, can be explained in part by how well they fit their surrounding conditions.

Governments that wish to introduce educational technology, then, must pay attention to the production function—to the critical surrounding conditions that are necessary to make the technology work.

IT ALL BEGINS WITH GOALS

I want to conclude simply by noting that economic analysis is very useful in understanding the choices a provider faces when considering the introduction of educational technology. But we need to remember also what economics, and technology, cannot do. They cannot establish objectives.

Education providers—usually governments—set the objectives. They decide whether costs are most important, or effectiveness, or efficiency. And they may well choose objectives that have not been mentioned here. For example, they may focus on equity rather than on efficiency. Or they may give priority to introducing a more modern, interactive pedagogical approach in classrooms, even if that is more costly and harder to evaluate.

Educational goals must drive technology decisions. Technology and economics are means, not ends.

The Half-life of Knowledge and Structural Reform of the Educational Sector

Today's dynamic globalizing economy, where the most important resource is the knowledge in the heads of the labor force, places increasing demands on educational systems already straining under the severe budgetary pressures faced by governments, enterprises, and families. The call everywhere is for

Peter T. Knight

increased coverage, better quality, and lifelong rather than terminal education. There is simply no way that these goals can be achieved without fundamentally re-inventing and re-engineering educational systems to reduce costs, increase efficiency, and lower prices.

Peter Knight is a partner in Knight, Moore—Telematics for Education and Development.

CHALLENGES FACING EDUCATIONAL POLICY AND FINANCE

Knowledge is exploding. In many countries the relative cost of education is rising. Even when citizens, business groups, and political leaders succeed in raising the social value placed on education—and hence the relative share of education in family, enterprise, municipal, state, and national budgets—resources are insufficient. A fundamental restructuring of educational systems is required to achieve what has been so elusive to date—a major increase in productivity.

The key is to mobilize more private sector finance and managerial skills and encourage the use of modern information and communications (telematics) technologies in education, both public and private. These technologies are reducing the cost of processing, storing, and transmitting knowledge at roughly 50 percent every 18 months. There is no end in sight to this dramatic fall in costs. The telematics revolution—fueled by digital, satellite, and fiber optic technologies and by the convergence of telecommunications, computers, and television—offers tremendous potential to reduce costs and increase productivity in education and training. But simply piling new technologies on top of old ones at every level of the system will not do.

What is needed is a thorough re-invention or re-engineering of the strategic education sector. The challenges are more organizational and political than technical. Competitive forces must be unleashed to push down prices to reflect the fall in costs. A wave of technological change is upon us, and the key to public policy is to manage the process of what Joseph Schumpeter called "creative destruction" to achieve clear national goals (Schumpeter, 1942). Countries, regions, cities, and companies which are able to create consensus around a vision of a strategically reformed education and training sector will be able to surf the wave of change and move ahead; those which do not are likely to be crushed by it. Families of future workers and individual workers already in the labor force also need to develop strategies to stay competitive in rapidly changing labor markets.

In the following sections I outline the key elements of educational and telecommunications policy reform, the concept of the "half-life of knowledge" (which I believe is helpful in deciding on how to organize and finance different parts of the educational system), key public policies which can encourage this reform, and the role of competition in driving technological change in the education and telecommunications sectors.

ELEMENTS OF EDUCATION, TRAINING, AND TELECOMMUNICATIONS POLICY REFORM

This restructuring and reform of educational systems is likely to involve increased provision of educational and training services by private sector training businesses and by enterprises providing training to their workers. Such private sector entities have strong incentives to provide knowledge which has immediate economic returns to the individuals and firms involved. These private sector enterprises are responsive to market forces, have strong incentives to increase efficiency and lower costs, and cannot survive providing training for outmoded skills or using obsolete equipment as often occurs in formal vocational training institutions. A recent World Bank study found, for example, that vocational education in Egypt has negative value added—it costs to unlearn the inappropriate skills being taught in such institutions.

Public education and training policy and appropriate economic incentives, including tax deductions and credits for the expenditures made, can stimulate private sector provision of education and training services.

But students and families often assess practical, vocational education as leading to a dead end. As a consequence, it is mostly students not qualifying for more academic training who tend to enroll in formal vocational training institutions. A key policy and regulatory reform is to establish what New Zealand (1990), Australia (1995), the United Kingdom, and now South Africa are calling a "national qualifications framework" (NQF). Under an NQF, knowledge is broken down into modules, and objective assessments of knowledge acquisition are made by certified testing authorities. (This can be done in many cases over the Internet using World Wide Web servers.) What is assessed is what the student knows, independently of how he or she acquired the knowledge. This opens the way to alternative providers of training, providers who compete on the basis of cost and quality objectively assessed through results (New Zealand Qualifications Authority, n.d.; Australian Qualifications Framework Advisory Board Secretariat, n.d.).

Independent study, study within formal educational institutions, on-the-job training provided by business enterprises, learning through specialized training firms, distance learning or classroom learning—in short, the learner will have multiple options to fit his or her budget, learning style, and opportunity cost of time used for study.

A complementary reform is the establishment, now being proposed in Korea, of an "educational credit bank," where students can accumulate credits from different educational service providers, and apply them toward various degrees or certificates. Students can "mix and match" credits obtained from public and private providers, theoretical/academic and practical/vocational knowledge. This innovation may allow flexibility, changes in direction over a lifetime rather than locking students into a single (often dead-end, terminal) educational path.

Finally, telecommunications policy reform is critical for accelerating productivity increase in education through lowering the costs of transmitting knowledge. Again the key is introducing competition and mobilizing private sector resources to lower prices in line with falling costs and mobilize needed investment capital, available from both domestic and international private sources. In many African countries, for example, waiting lists for even outrageously high-priced conventional telephone service from under-financed public sector monopoly providers is from five to ten years. Providing broadly available Internet service in these conditions is a pipe dream. This obvious mismatch between demand and supply can only be broken by regulatory reform. This requires mobilizing the education, health, business and other constituencies being harmed by the inefficient state monopolies. To paraphrase Clauswitz, telecommunications policy is too important to be left solely in the hands of the existing monopoly providers (UNECA, 1997; Knight, 1995).

A possible use for public subsidies is to encourage development of the physical infrastructure necessary for distance learning throughout a national territory (e.g. Internet backbone development, as has been done in the United States and Brazil). This does not mean the state itself must build and operate such infrastructure—in fact a good case to the contrary can be made for competitive provision by private sector enterprises.

THE HALF-LIFE OF KNOWLEDGE, THE RATE OF KNOWLEDGE ACQUISITION, AND ALTERNATIVE DELIVERY MODES

What kinds of knowledge lend themselves best to different types of educational service provision and finance? I propose a distinction between short half-life knowledge (SHK) and long half-life knowledge

(LHK). Their respective characteristics are summarized in the table on the next page. Table 1 emphasizes the speed of acquisition and deterioration of long as opposed to short half-life knowledge. Of course these are the polar extremes; much knowledge may lie somewhere between them on a continuum.

LHK tends to take years, or at best months to acquire, and it has a much slower rate of depreciation than SHK. LHK lends itself to systematic acquisition over a number of years in formal educational institutions. LHK also tends to have what economists call "positive externalities" (economic or social benefits accruing to society and not just to the individual receiving it—consider the examples of basic language, acculturation, socialization, and citizenship skills). It includes many technical areas, such as the traditional mechanical and electrical trades (as well as many others), which take a long time to master, are very expensive, and require a solid theoretical and conceptual basis. But it would exclude specializations within these same trades (such as MIG welding within the mechanical trades) because they take little time to master and become obsolete when newer processes appear. LHK also is a good candidate for public sector finance and provision as well. Since the economic returns are not immediate, LHK is most often financed by families and by the state rather than by active members of the labor force or companies in which they are working.

SHK, on the other hand, can often be acquired in a matter of days,

Table 1. Attributes of long half-life knowledge and short half-life knowledge

	Long Half-Life Knowledge	Short Half-Life Knowledge
Knowledge Type	Academic, basic, theoretical, complex trades	Short—vocational, practical
Acquisition Time	Long—years, months	Short—days, weeks, months
Quick Econ. Return	No	Yes
Social Externalities	High	Low
Finance	Families, state	Workers, businesses
Examples	Basic socialization, citizenship, language, mathematics, logic, reasoning, theoretical parts of professional training	Industrial processes, software use, specific technical and professional skills

weeks, or at most months. It tends to be practical, highly specialized vocational knowledge, or simple trades such as hair cutting, and as such has a quick economic return. Often it depreciates rapidly—its useful life is short. Consider, for example, learning to perform a specific industrial process, use a new piece of software, or perform a new surgical technique. If not practiced quickly, the knowledge is easily forgotten. In any case, since technological progress is rapid in many fields (even if practiced), the knowledge is likely to become obsolete quickly—again consider the examples of industrial processes, software, or surgical techniques. What is "state-of-the-art" cutting-edge knowledge providing the holder a competitive edge today is likely to become economically outmoded (depreciated or rendered obsolete) by technological progress tomorrow. This kind of knowledge is an excellent candidate for private sector provision and finance by individual members of the labor force or companies. Public finance (say through tax credits or other fiscal stimuli, or through the distribution of "training vouchers" to be used by individuals choosing among competing providers of education and training services) may be relevant if there are also social benefits beyond those accruing to individuals and/or the firms in which they work.

A good case for public finance, perhaps from employment taxes, may be made for acquisition of new skills by workers rendered unemployed through technological change or international trade which makes their skills and the products of the enterprises where they have been employed obsolete or non-competitive. While technological change produces overall social benefits, the process of "creative destruction" tends to render obsolete older technologies and the skills specific to them. The task for public policy, for families, for enterprises, and for individual workers is to move "upstream" into skills appropriate for "sunrise" rather than "sunset" industries.

A working hypothesis is that SHK lends itself to private sector provision and finance, whereas LHK, which is necessary for the acquisition of many kinds of short half-life knowledge, is better adapted to public sector finance and provision. Rapid technological change to take advantage of the information and communication technology revolution is most likely to occur fastest in the provision of SHK in the competitive private sector. But the fall in the prices of educational services which competition makes possible can put competitive pressure on traditional formal educational sector institutions providing LHK, in both the public and private sector.

A more radical view is that the public sector should not directly provide vocational training in public institutions, but leave it to enterprises and individuals to finance the acquisition of such knowledge, since it is in their interest to do so. This will save scarce public funding for LHK with high social externalities, which is less likely to be financed by private sector firms or individuals in the socially desirable quantities.

Public sector provision of vocational education often leads to inferior students acquiring outdated technical skills using obsolescent or obsolete machinery and software. Public funding may be appropriate to encourage provision of needed skills, as in the case of workers rendered unemployed by technological change or international trade in "sunset" industries. But it is better to allow workers and enterprises to choose their own providers of such training, whether private or public institutions, perhaps by distributing "retraining vouchers" to the affected workers. The state can encourage high-quality provision by certifying providers and establishing more generally a regulatory framework which encourages competition in the provision of such services, including by setting standards and mechanisms for assessing whether the knowledge has been obtained.

Today the quality assurance function is mostly performed by certifying the quality of training institutions, which themselves administer the formal assessments (examinations, tests) subject to various quality checks. But a promising route for the future is to encourage the establishment of independent assessment centers, which may function over the Internet or via physical centers. The Educational Testing Service in the US performs this function for some academic skills (e.g., the Scholastic Aptitude Test, the Graduate Record Examination, and the Test of English as a Foreign Language), and the European Union is planning to establish such assessment centers for a variety of academic disciplines.

COSTS, PRICES, COMPETITION, AND TECHNOLOGICAL CHANGE IN EDUCATION

The key to achieving needed productivity increase in the education sector is to harness the information and communications (telematics) technology revolution. But introducing revolutionary new technologies in rigid, conservative, unionized, and bureaucratized structures is difficult, to say the least. Such structures are all too common in the formal education sector providing LHK, especially the public parts. It is much easier in the competitive, private sector providing SHK.

Enterprises in this sector must either meet market tests of value, efficiency, and timeliness, or die. It is thus no surprise that it is in the competitive, private subsector that the adoption of telematics in education is proceeding most rapidly.

In industry, "just-in-time" production has drastically reduced costs by virtually eliminating inventories. Now "just-in-time" training is becoming the norm, minimizing the "stockpiling" of fast-depreciating knowledge in the labor force. Education and training on demand—anywhere, anytime—is now technically feasible, and costs are falling fast. Global and regional as well as national markets for education and training are developing rapidly.

I believe it is in the competitive market for SHK that we may expect costs (including the cost of knowledge depreciation) to be most closely controlled, and prices to fall most rapidly. The forces of "creative destruction" unleashed by the telematics revolution can push down prices to reflect sharply declining costs of processing, storing, and transmitting knowledge because competitive producers cannot charge monopoly rents. If these producers do not lower prices to reflect falling costs, they will be displaced in the market by training firms which do lower prices. Thus, establishing a competitive marketplace for training and education services should be a major objective of government policy in the education sector.

Competitive pressures can also be brought to bear in the market for LHK if a proper regulatory framework and other elements of an incentive structure are put in place. We are already beginning to see this happen in university-level education, where costs have exploded along with knowledge. In the US, for example, the cost to a family of sending a child to college (including tuition, room, and board) is approaching 15 percent of median family income for a public university, up from 9 percent 15 years ago. For private universities, the figure has doubled to 40 percent of medium family income over the same 15-year period (Daniel, 1997). Private firms such as Motorola, ATT, and IBM are establishing their own virtual universities for staff training, and other private firms, such as Jones Education, are opening global virtual universities open to the public.

There are two main ways in which the cost of university education can be reduced. The first is organizational change—exemplified by the pioneering British Open University (BOU). Established in 1969, in 1995 it had over 157,000 students in degree programs, at an average cost per student 50 percent of that in other U.K. universities (Daniel, 1997, Table 2). Evaluations indicate that the quality of education provided by BOU is at least as good if not better. The secret lies in the large returns to scale being reaped in course design to high quality standards and the provision of multimedia instruction (offering the student options in learning from text, video, tutors, audio cassette and now over the Internet). The high fixed costs are spread over a huge spatially dispersed student body, resulting in lower average costs per student and greater ability of students to use the learning tools which best suit individual learning styles. And all this has been achieved at a public institution where fees paid by students account for only 31 percent of university income. Now BOU is moving rapidly to take advantage of the second source of cost reductions—technological change. Through its new Knowledge Media Institute it is rapidly incorporating Internet and other computer-based technologies into its panoply of instructional tools.

In Latin America there are a number of open universities inspired by the British model, but it is the Virtual University of Monterrey (part of the System of the Technological Institute of Monterey - ITESM) in Mexico which is the largest (over 43,000 students in 26 Mexican campuses), most international (providing instruction in 13 universities in 6 countries and planning on expanding further), and most technologically advanced (using television, Internet, and 2-way videoconferencing delivered by satellite) (Rectoria de la Universidad Virtual, n.d.). While costs at this private institution are not yet lower than conventional universities, as the student base expands this may become the case as high fixed costs are spread over a broader student population.

Another good example of the use of technology in formal education in Latin America—this time primary and secondary school education targeted at 15-30 year-olds already in the labor force—is the Fundação Roberto Marinho's Telecurso 2000, delivered by television and print materials to an audience in the millions every day in Brazil (Fundação Roberto Marinho, n.d.; Oliveira, 1997; Knight 1996). Importantly, this program was developed by a private foundation and financed by the Federation of Industries of São Paulo State (FIESP), but it is increasingly being used in public primary and secondary schools. Educational programming including the Telecurso 2000 is now being delivered direct to home by satellite on a special educational channel (TV Futura).

TV Futura should shortly have competition from a second Portuguese language direct-to-home educational channel being established by the Abril group as part of the Direct TV Latin America consortium (Galaxy Latin America, or GLA). GLA is already offering an educational channel in Spanish (Cl@se-Canal Latinoamericano de Servicios Educativos).

In Brazil, Chile, Costa Rica, Jamaica, and Mexico, major programs are now underway with government support to bring computers to the classroom of public as well as private schools. There is already a good deal of experience accumulated in the United States (Conte, 1997) and other countries as well. There are ample opportunities in Latin America to link up with private providers of video-based content such as TV Futuro and Cl@se in new public/private sector partnerships, as is already happening in some Brazilian states. The public sector is also active in content provision via television, e.g., Mexico's Telesecundaria (now exporting programs to Central America), and Brazil's TV Escola.

Educational television is an area where Latin America is a world leader, and strong economic arguments can be made for giving priority to exploiting this existing comparative advantage (Castro, 1997). But given the rapid development of wireless technologies, which permit more personalized and interactive approaches, it is important to at least experiment in the use of Internet and other computer-based training and education technologies to complement television. Interestingly, Brazil's Telecurso 2000 is now moving to develop complementary Internet-based instruction and support Fundação Roberto Marinho, n.d.) to its televised programs and print-based instruction. Likewise, Mexico's Telesecundária is integrating its offerings with the new Red Escolar, both of which are operated by the Instituto Latinoamericano de la Comunicacion Educativa (ILCE).

New Technologies for Professional Education, Training, and Human Resource Development
What Works; What Makes Sense?

T his section presents a brief synthesis of current uses of computers and telecommunications in education and training. Its focus is the use of computer networks in

Alexander J. Romiszowski

professional education, in corporate training and in human resource development.

COMPUTERS AND NETWORKS IN EDUCATION

Computer-mediated communication (CMC) for group-learning

Computer mediated communication (CMC) is a generic term used to describe any system which enables people to communicate with other people by means of computer networks. Well-known examples include computer conferencing, electronic mail, discussion lists, listserves and bulletin board systems. In education and training, CMC systems are used to implement discussions organized in a manner very similar to conventional classrooms, thus creating a form of "virtual classroom"

Dr. Romiszowski is on the faculties of the School of Education, Syracuse University and the School of the Future, University of São Paulo

(Hiltz, 1986; 1990). Other uses are seminars mediated by computers, case study discussions mediated by computers, and on-line equivalents of other small-group discussion methodologies (Romiszowski, Jost & Chang, 1990; Romiszowski, 1993).

Computer-mediated information, or instruction, for individual learning

Another function of computer networks is to gain access to remote databases, to consult electronic libraries or to transmit information to workers at the workplace. Generally, such information may not be used for group discussion or argumentation between people, but rather by individuals for their own purposes. Examples include on-line journals, electronic or virtual libraries, access to interactive data banks such as the Dow Jones Index on the stock exchange, and electronic banking systems.

Yet another form of educational use of computers is *computer assisted instruction* (CAI) or *computer-based training* (CBT). It comes in various forms but always with the intention of promoting specific learning through interaction with software rather than with teachers or other people involved in the learning process. The tendency is for the individual to study independently using software stored in computers or networks.

Integrated systems

Recently many examples of educational applications have appeared that involve a combination of information and instruction dissemination systems, such as CAI or CBT, with facilities for group discussion on the same computer network (Romiszowski & Chang, 1992). Such integrated systems of computer delivery and support of collaborative work are the basis of the current movement towards "telework" and "virtual groups" in the business context. They are becoming more common in education and training contexts. In the work context, this tendency is often referred to as *computer-supported cooperative* work or CSCW (Grief, 1988). In the context of education, the parallel phenomenon is often referred to as *computer-supported collaborative learning* or CSCL (Kaye, 1992).

Other integrated systems appearing in the work context with ever greater frequency are the so-called *electronic performance support systems* (EPSS). This type of system supplies the worker at his or her work station (which now typically is a computer attached to a network) with all the information and access to other specialists who might be necessary to consult in order to get the work done in the most cost-effective manner. Use of these systems is growing so fast that it is considered by some authors to represent a new paradigm for human resources development (Gery, 1991). One trend which is now in current fashion and which includes EPSS as at least one of its forms is "just-in-time training" (Lewis & Romiszowski, 1995).

Another recent movement is the trend towards computer-based multimedia systems for education, training and human resource development. These may be encountered as stand-alone instructional or informational systems (perhaps in CD-ROMs), as databases on a network, or as elements within audiographic computer conferencing systems and group discussion environments involving visual and audio support (such as desktop video).

The variety of different forms of CAI, CBT, CMC, CSCW and EPSS which are now in use is very large. In this paper, the focus is limited to those approaches that have already been implemented with success and which have generated a reasonable quantity of research. This will enable us to evaluate the potential impact of these new technologies in the real world of education and training.

WHY DO WE NEED COMPUTERS AND NETWORKS IN EDUCATION?

In this section, we present two lines of argument that support the use of new technologies, particularly networking technologies, as essential "survival strategies" of future education and training systems.

Current educational trends

Until quite recently, the major activity in software development for education and training worked within the paradigm of individual learning toward precisely defined goals. This is the conventional model of CAI or CBT. However, there is a growing tendency toward more use of computers in networks to promote group learning activities. This is for a combination of reasons that include technological developments related to access to computer networks as well as socioeconomic developments related to the type of work people perform and the skills they need. The current Internet technology and the forthcoming higher speed and broader band technologies promised by future information superhighways make possible distance learning activities that model very closely the interactive group learning activities that have been the mainstay of much of conventional education in the past.

The socioeconomic developments are in part a reaction to the impact of technology on society. They are creating a situation in which just to be employable, people must continually upgrade their knowledge and skills and be active learners, active problem solvers and active critical thinkers. In the development of these generic skills of learning and of thinking, the methodologies of education put more stress on group activities as opposed to individual learning activities.

Thus we see a confluence of technological, sociological and psychological reasons for the current trend which is moving the use of computer technology in education and training from individualized self-learning models to distance-delivered group-learning models.

Two problems: population and education

In addition to the technological and pedagogical arguments just presented, there is another way to look at future demand for education and the role of technologies in meeting that demand. We can compare educational demand (the problem of education) with the demand for food which Malthus in the 19th century referred to as the problem of population. He predicted great tragedies for humanity as a result of the exponential growth in population related to the linear growth in the capacity of societies to produce food.

However, looking back from the 20th century, although there are places in the world where there is hunger, the situation has not become as dramatic and tragic as Malthus predicted. The reason for this is that the agricultural community managed to create an exponential growth in food production directly through the application of new technologies to agriculture. In the same way, we might today predict a great tragedy in the area of education and culture if the current systems and methods of teaching and learning do not recreate themselves to meet the exponentially growing needs for education and training. Using the problem of population as an analogy, we could argue that the only route to increasing the supply of education proportionate to the increasing demand is through the systematic and rational application of new information technologies to the process.

Extending our analogy, we may observe that in the area of agriculture there were many local disasters, both ecological and sociological, largely created by the inappropriate or unintelligent application of technologies. Most of these disasters could have been avoided if the innovative projects in the area of agriculture had been planned, implemented, controlled and evaluated more carefully. In the same way, we can argue that not all innovative projects applying new technologies to education are likely to be successful. However, through systematic planning, controlled implementation and continuous evaluation of the projects, we can hope to increase the probability of success. The bottom line is that we have to innovate and risk some failures or suffer the certainty of a generalized disaster.

NEW SYSTEMS FOR COMMUNICATION AND EDUCATION

This section reviews some of the trends and innovations underway which promise to drastically modify nearly all of the axioms that we currently accept as the basis for our education, training and human resource development systems.

The nature of work

In the world of information, the machine is encroaching more every day on the areas of work which traditionally have been carried out by human beings. Robots take over the physical work of operators in factories. Software applications and intelligent expert systems are taking over a large part of the routine intellectual tasks that human beings have traditionally carried out. What is remaining for the human being are those types of activities that computers and information technology are not (or shall we say, not yet) good at performing—namely, the more creative and inventive forms of work. This involves critical problem analysis, formulation of important problems, prioritization of problems, a search for information that might be relevant to their solution, creation of original and innovative solutions, and then the implementation and troubleshooting of these solutions in innovative pilot projects of an innovative nature.

It follows that education must lay ever-increasing emphasis on the development of creative thinking and productive thinking skills and less on the acquisition of specific content related to a particular job. Content is subject to flux and change due to the rapid evolution of the workplace. The worker must continually update himself or herself in relation to this content as part of a continuing education process that occurs beyond basic schooling, higher education and formal professional education. These changes in the reality of work in society imply quite important changes in both the content and the methods of education for the next century.

Virtual work groups

The methods of teaching and learning typically used in mediated (computer or television) courses in the past are not the most appropriate methods for the development of critical and creative thinking skills. Research and practical experience show that such skills are more effectively developed in small group discussion activities such as the case study method, debates and brainstorming sessions, or in group project work of various types. In the world of the future, people will need to develop these skills to a higher level than in the past. But as the costs of group meetings is every day greater in comparison to the falling costs of telecommunication, the opportunities for the appropriate types of educational activity could become scarcer rather than more available. We may face the paradox in which in education, and particularly in higher education and continuing adult education, we have less and less opportunity to engage in the types of learning activities that we more and more require.

Given that these conditions are at least in part being created by the impact of technology on the world of work and on society, it would appear appropriate to turn to technology for a solution to the problem it is creating. One approach to a solution is to develop technology-based methods of replicating or even exceeding the effectiveness and efficiency of small-group discussion methods as they have been practiced in the classroom in the past. This is the impetus behind the current plethora of research and development projects in the area of on-line education (Romiszowski & Mason, 1996).

Performance support systems

Another important trend is the avoidance of unnecessary learning of content that is used only occasionally and for short periods before it is obsolete, substituting learning by reference on the job at the required time to well-designed information sources and performance support systems. The computer is rapidly becoming the universal work tool, present on everybody's desktop or alongside everybody's machine, serving as a communication center, control center, support center, and so on. Why should it not also be used as a general purpose teaching machine, bringing to the worker at the workplace all the information and access to all of the expertise which is necessary in order to perform the work effectively and efficiently?

Indeed, such electronic performance systems are being developed and implemented with increasing frequency by many business organizations, transforming the role of training and human resource development. We are, in a way, moving back to conditions that are similar to the Middle Ages master-apprentice relationship where the apprentice would learn on the job under the supervision of a master craftsman, permanently available at the workplace. However, today, the master is no longer a physically present human being but an electronic system which encapsulates the knowledge of the master and which, to some extent, may embody also some of the skills of analysis and evaluation that a master would utilize to orient an apprentice. Furthermore, the system acts as a communication network to enable the apprentice to access human support from real master performers when and if required.

Just-in-time training

The rapid diversification and evolution of work methodologies and short shelf-life of new products and services are creating a situation in which the conventional approaches to training and education for business no longer meet the needs. It is not efficient to learn large quantities of information off the job in courses prior to work when, by the time work commences, much of that information is already obsolete. Furthermore, it is not efficient to bring groups of people together for courses that have a standard content and curriculum when those people, although they may hold the same job titles, are probably using different information for different purposes in their day-to-day work. Each professional therefore requires individualized treatment in the planning of continuing education and training in order to keep up with the changes in the workplace.

To implement such an individualized approach, we need, in the first place, to involve the adult professional in the planning of his or her own program of self development. Secondly, this program should be available to the individual exactly when that individual requires it in order to upgrade or refresh his or her skills. For both of these reasons, the conventional structure of institutionalized higher education and especially technical education cannot meet the needs of our future clientele. This is leading to the creation of new alternatives for technical and higher education which are very much under user control and available to each user on demand. These systems have been christened "just-in-time training."

It is interesting to note here the emphasis on individualization of the process of planning the content, methods and timing of the program, contrasted to the non-individualization of the learning process itself when that learning process is trying to develop critical thinking and creative problem-solving skills. We have here some interesting problems to solve in the design of future continuing adult education systems. Just-in-time training is often perceived as a highly individualized self-study process. However, it should be considered as only partly so, with another (possibly greater and growing) part being the flexible provision of just-in-time group interaction opportunities.

The importance of distance education

One approach to dealing with the somewhat paradoxical situation mentioned above is through the use of distance education systems as opposed to institutionalized place-based educational systems. Such systems may be built to allow on-demand access to specific modules of learning as required by individuals. Another benefit of such a system is the ability to create groups of like-minded individuals with similar needs and interests who may not necessarily reside or work in one and the same place.

This new set of needs may be one of the factors behind the obvious trend toward distance education at all levels of the formal education system (with the possible exception of elementary education). Some researchers are estimating that in the area of higher education, for example, we will not be far into the next century before there will be more students studying at a distance than studying at conventional university campuses. It is very probable that such trends will occur even faster in technical and vocational education, not necessarily through elimination of all initial basic training courses but rather to provide continuing education for keeping up with the changing realities of work.

One innovative approach involves the emphasis on structuring content so that users may find what they require and at the level of difficulty and detail that suits them, within a domain of knowledge on a particular technical area. Such systems may combine hypertext and hypermedia, carefully developed and structured, with techniques such as information mapping (Horn, 1989) that are associated with group collaborative work. Computer mediated communication systems are used to supplement instruction with exercises that stretch people's creative abilities and share experience among individuals (Romiszowski & Corso, 1990). These trends underlie the current debate about virtual schools and virtual universities.

Technological synergy

Another important trend is the technological synergy occurring between ideas springing from computer science, the telecommunication sciences, and the areas of psychology and cognitive science. This synergy is creating a whole new range of possibilities such as software which can act as "intelligent agents" or "intelligent interfaces" between knowledge bases and the users, facilitating both the localization and the intelligent use of information. Possibilities which are just around the corner include the instantaneous automatic translation of information from one language to another. This would allow not only access to materials generated in other languages but even group collaborative work involving participants who do not speak the same language. Another area of research showing as yet unrealized potential is "virtual reality." This research is working toward the creation of on-line "virtual" environments that in time are expected to be almost undistinguishable from real environments.

The implementation of such technologies could signify the end of "distance education" as a useful term, in that the distinction between education at a distance and not at a distance may vanish completely. We can imagine future CMC systems that are not subject to current limitations regarding the loss of non-verbal communication through expressions, tone of voice, gestures, and even physical contact, which in many cases play important roles in conventional education activities. Such ideas may seem to verge on science fiction at this time, but the progress in these areas of synergy of the sciences is so rapid that some practical applications will, without doubt, soon appear. These innovations may further revolutionize the way we envisage the teaching/learning process.

The philosophical and theoretical viewpoint

We may conclude this section by reflecting on how the theoreticians in psychology, sociology and the philosophy of education are viewing these technological developments. One aspect that has always been a characteristic of educational thinking is the diversity of often conflicting paradigms and theories. Educators have never converged on one single theory of education or indeed of teaching and learning. A review of the variety of approaches may be found on the Internet (http://gwis2.crcirc.gwu.edu/kearsley). Here Kearsley presents a review of no less than 48 different theories of learning. Another source that illustrates the variety is the recently published book *Instructional Development Paradigms* (Dills & Romiszowski, 1997).

One current debate which seems to have a lot of relevance for a discussion of computers and networks in education is the so-called debate between constructivism and objectivism. The constructivist point of view is frequently favorable to computer mediated communication, and not so favorable to computer assisted instruction (Cunningham, Duffy & Knuth, 1993). Other writers, without getting involved in the theoretical debate of constructivism versus objectivism, defend the appropriate uses of CMC for some categories of learning and of CAI for others. This approach is an extension of the relatively conventional and well-tried methodologies of instructional design that seek to use a taxonomic system of categorization of the content or objectives of a given course as a step towards the selection of methods and media. It is possible to see this extension in terms of either a broadening of the definition of the term "instruction" or the addition of another term, which I choose to refer to as "conversation" (Romiszowski & Lewis, 1995).

In general, it is possible to conclude that the use of computer networks for education and training has support for one reason or another from most of the philosophical and theoretical viewpoints currently held in the education field.

HOW DO WE USE COMPUTERS AND NETWORKS IN EDUCATION?

Historical antecedents

In reality, computer mediated communication is one of the oldest forms of computer use in the educational context. This use began as a spin-off from the US program that installed ARPANET as part of the development of secure communication systems in the event of nuclear war. ARPANET was planned to offer multiple channels of communication between the points of the network so that if part of the network were defective or destroyed, messages could still travel between the nodes of the unaffected part by alternative routes (Elmer-Dewitt, 1994). This network became used for research purposes and then through the National Science Foundation was transformed into NSFNET. In time it became available to most universities, research units and many other scientific organizations.

The democratization of access to the networks

The linking of an ever-greater number of local area and regional networks to this government network created an ever more complex and more distributed communication network involving increasing numbers of computer users. This is how the Internet came about. This powerful "network of networks" has become an indispensable tool for research and collaborative work in the scientific community. However, in recent years, the academic exclusivity of the Internet has been broken down as an increasing number of commercial Internet access providers have facilitated use of the network by any person who so wishes and has access to a computer and modem. As millions of users joined the Internet fraternity, we began to see a transformation in the communication habits of North American society and in time of most other countries. It is not surprising, therefore, that one of the major areas of research on technology in education is focused on the use of computer mediated communication methodologies based on the Internet and its user-friendly hypermedia interface, the World Wide Web (Khan, 1996).

CMC in the business world

Computer mediated communication is already firmly established in the business community as a viable, often preferred, method of communication. Most major companies today, in the United States and Europe as well as in many other places, maintain their own networks to facilitate effective and efficient communication between departments, whether these departments are in one geographical place or distributed across the country. In these systems, the use of electronic mail and computer conferencing has increased as a means of economically carrying on business and as an alternative to meetings, which are fixed in both time and geographical location. This is one factor in the so-called globalization of business communication which is already becoming essential for many companies in order to maintain competitiveness in the information society. Once this new communication infrastructure is in place, it is natural that it should also be used for training, human resource development and indeed the avoidance of formal training through the use of on-the-job performance support systems.

CMC in education and training

In education and training, the major area of innovation in recent years is the use of computer mediated communication systems, not only for distance education when people are physically separated but also for more convenient communication between people who work and live in the same locale but have different schedules. Many studies have shown that such use can greatly increase the efficiency and effectiveness of conventional campus-based university education (Grabowski, Suciati & Pusch, 1990).

In the area of distance education, the potential savings in terms of time, transport costs, space, electrical energy, heating, even professors' salaries in some cases, are combining to make distance education an exceedingly attractive alternative to conventional approaches. As the technologies enable the teaching/learning activities orchestrated at a distance to evermore approximate those that can be implemented in classroom settings, the economic factors are strongly influencing administrators to seek to implement distance education whenever possible.

The Net as a distance training system: some case examples

Example 1: Internal training in the company

The trends in the business world mentioned above are now percolating into the area of training and development of human resources. For example, a few years ago, the North American telephone company AT&T introduced the use of teleconferencing methods for training in place of conventional courses. This trend grew so that today, just a few years later, the majority of AT&T training is performed across its "Teletraining Network." In 1989, for example, more than 69,000 employees participated at least once during the year in some form of teleconference-based training activities. In general, the results have been most satisfactory: very substantial reductions in training cost without any apparent reductions in training effectiveness (Chute, 1990).

We may note, therefore, that this rapid expansion in electronic training at AT&T has been a response not so much to the greater effectiveness of these methods but to their economic appeal. AT&T reports training cost reduction on the order of 60 percent per student hour of participation. This reduction has been gained almost entirely by a reduction in travel and travel-related costs. Another part of the savings has come from a reduction in time lost and productivity lost, as people used to spend two or three days away from work to participate in a single day of training (Chute, 1988, 1990).

Example 2: Formal State provision of distance training

An illustrative contrast can be drawn between New Zealand and the State of New York. I have chosen these two cases because of their similarities in geography and population size. Excluding the large urban area of New York City, the population of New York State is principally rural, distributed in small communities or on farms. Access to basic education opportunities is difficult for many state residents. These same factors are found in New Zealand.

New Zealand began in the 1930s to incorporate a "Correspondence School" for primary and secondary schooling as part of its formal national educational system. It also has operated a distance-teaching technical school since the 1940s, originally named the "Technical Correspondence Institute" but recently re-christened the "Technical Open Polytechnic." These two institutions are the largest of their category in the country. The number of students studying at a distance through the Correspondence School is several times greater than the number of students at the largest conventional school in the country. The New Zealand Technical Open Polytechnic, or "TOP," has received an annual average of more than 95,000 students a year throughout the 1970s and 1980s, which represents about 3 percent of the total population of the country and 30 percent of all the technical students in the country. The other 70 percent are distributed across another 12 conventional technical colleges (Nicoll, 1987).

The New York State educational system has never operated or financially supported any specific distance education institution. However, recent statistics show that at present the state indirectly supports more than 200 separate small projects. These have been set up by conventional institutions, (schools, colleges, universities, and so on) and are utilizing distance education methods (principally through electronic communication networks) for certain aspects of their activities. For example, three conventional schools in different municipalities might share the services of a specialist technical or language teacher, thus forming a virtual group of students across the three campuses that is sufficiently large to justify the teacher's salary. These small projects hardly existed at the beginning of the 1980s. But there were more than 100 such projects publicly supported in New York State by 1990, and more than 200 by 1995. Although the individual projects are all small and independent, they add up to a significant level of official support of distance education by the state.

The new electronic communication technologies are capable of making the use of distance education economically viable on a small scale as well as pedagogically desirable in the context of conventional education. Indeed, the differentiation between conventional educational institutions and distance educational institutions may soon disappear. The case of New Zealand illustrates this trend. The Technical Open Polytechnic is entering into a crisis of downsizing as its student enrollment diminishes annually. This is not the result of a reduction in the popularity of distance education or of some geographic or demographic changes within New Zealand; it is the result of a combination of political changes implemented by recent governments and the socioeconomic impact of new technologies.

For some years now, the New Zealand government has been transforming its concept of education "as a free service to all citizens" into a system that must be economically viable and self-financing. They use the term "user pays" for this policy. This has made all educational institutions much more cost-conscious and competitive. All institutions are beginning to use electronic communication methods for administration and distance teaching, especially when these methods can lead to improved viability and cost-effectiveness. The result of this is that the other twelve technical colleges in New Zealand have become competitors for the same body of students that the Polytechnic has traditionally serviced (Rajasingham, Nicoll & Romiszowski, 1992).

THE FUTURE: CHANGE IN THE ROLE OF PROFESSIONAL TRAINING AND EDUCATION

Given the trends and scenarios described in this paper, it is not surprising that the concept of self-development is taking root as a major paradigm for human resource development in industry and business. This paradigm emphasizes that the responsibility to keep oneself updated and employable rests with each employee. The employer's responsibility is to make the process of self-learning viable—helping in the identification of individual learning needs and facilitating access to the resources necessary to satisfy those needs.

This reality reduces the relevance of setting up standardized training courses along traditional lines (whether set up by the company itself or by external course providers). The tendency, instead, is toward the greater use of communication networks to access databanks and virtual libraries, and the formation of virtual groups of students with similar needs and interests who may collaborate at a distance or may help each other in self-development activities of various forms (Eurich, 1990).

This tendency grew first in the area of business education and training, but today is also spreading to the general area of higher education. It is one factor responsible for reductions in the number of students applying to conventional undergraduate programs in campus-based universities. Many graduates find that they seldom or never catch up with their peers who went straight into employment and then completed their studies on a part-time basis through night school or, increasingly, through distance education opportunities.

We may be seeing a transformation in the culture of formal higher education with vast repercussions in the very near future. A recent pronouncement by Peter Drucker quoted in an interview with *Forbes* Magazine gives conventional campus-based universities only a few short years before they become completely obsolete. In addition to mentioning the trends we have outlined above, Drucker points out that the costs of conventional university education in the United States have been increasing along a curve that is similar to the increasing cost of Medicare as the population of the country ages. He asserts that this is untenable over the medium- and long-term and therefore that the system will completely break down unless it drastically transforms itself. He sees this transformation as being largely toward network-based higher education.

These last points alert us to the importance of looking carefully at the best means of providing appropriate educational experiences of high quality and effectiveness to students who opt, or are forced, to study via networks instead of through conventional campus-based courses. The focus here should be on the research and development of methodologies that can replicate within networks the strong points of place-based conventional education. The current diversification of needs, and the heightened importance of critical and creative thinking for human beings who do not wish to be replaced by robots and expert systems, compel us to focus our attention on developing what we might call "conversational design" principles and methodologies.

Our networks enable us to converse with our peers at a distance in a relatively natural manner, particularly as multimedia video conferencing is implemented into what was previously text-based electronic communication. However, there is much still left to learn about how to devise effective and efficient learning environments within these contexts. Some research has recently been done on the principles of developing conversational learning environments on electronic networks (e.g., Romiszowski & Chang, 1992; Chang, 1994). However, this is an area of educational research that still requires considerable attention and that might be considered a top priority for educational technology research in the next few years.

The world is changing at such a rate that we do not have many years in which to avoid the "problem of education" that was mentioned at the beginning of this paper as analogous to the "problem of population" postulated by Malthus over a hundred years ago.

Instructional Technology—Then and Now

In 1974, Wilbur Schramm and others at Stanford University completed a major study on instructional technology. While it is more than 20 years old, the conclusions of that study may still be relevant.

Laurence Wolff

Below is a matrix of conclusions from that study compared to tentative conclusions for 1997.

LEARNING

1974	1997
Students usually learned as much from an instructional technology as from classroom teaching (this applied to cognitive skills only).	This continues to be true, but there are now elements of curriculum which may be taught more effectively by technology than by conventional instruction (e.g., simulations, foreign language)

Laurence Wolff works for the Education Unit of the Inter-American Development Bank.

1974	1997
There was no general learning superiority for one type of technology over another.	This still appears to be true. However it may be that interactive technologies (e.g. Internet, CD-ROM) will be found to be more effective than traditional radio and television (but these can simulate interactivity.)
The addition of another channel of instruction, for example print plus television, usually improved instruction.	Still true. Now defined as multi-channel instruction.
Motivated students learned from any instructional technology if it was competently used and adapted to their needs	Still true

COST OF DIFFERENT TECHNOLOGIES

1974	1997
The costs of instructional television (ITV) ranged from $.015 to $.15 per student served. The lower limit could be reached if a million students were located in a relatively small region. The costs of instructional radio were about one fifth the costs of television	Hardware and communication costs, especially of radio and television, have declined significantly and will continue to decline.
Computer aided instruction (CAI) was so expensive that it was not feasible except on a pilot basis.	Costs of computers have declined so much that generalized instruction by computers is now feasible. Off-the-shelf software especially for drill and practice is now inexpensive. Nonetheless costs are still significant and investment tradeoffs must be made.

1974	1997
Inexpensive technologies, especially radio, were as cost-effective as more expensive technologies.	This is still true.
	A third media channel (Internet), in addition to radio and television, is now available with its own particular cost structure.

TECHNOLOGY FOR EXTENDING THE SCHOOL (E.G., DISTANCE EDUCATION)

1974	1997
Students usually learned as much from distance programs as from conventional instruction.	This remains true. In addition, there may now be elements of curriculum which can be taught more effectively by technology than by conventional instruction.
These programs cost less than conventional classroom instruction.	Cost savings through distance education should be even greater than in the past.
Distance education programs offered opportunities which would normally not be available because of cost, logistics, or staffing problems. They were usually successful because separate and new institutions were established.	The increased number of instructional technology options means that there are even more opportunities than before, especially in higher education, for distance education.

1974	1997
The high visibility of an instructional technology, when it was used to provide a significant portion of curriculum content, made it a strong catalyst for curriculum and pedagogical reform.	This continues to be true. Instructional technology can play a major role in achieving curriculum reform objectives such as increased higher order cognitive skills. Also, there is now an opportunity to make the teacher less of a provider of knowledge and more a manager of learning, increasingly focusing for example on motivation and on remediation.
To be successful, technology programs required strong support from the top, acceptance and understanding by teachers, focused usage, integration into the overall system of instruction, and phased introduction, as a means of overcoming bureaucratic and pedagogical conservatism.	These steps continue to be fundamental to ensure success of technology projects.
No direct cost savings through technology were identified.	While start-up costs are significant, there is growing evidence that total costs can be reduced through increased learning, reduced repetition, and possibly higher student teacher ratios.
There were few demonstrable effects on learning when technology was used to "enrich" curriculum which was teacher provided.	This is probably also the case now.

1974	1997
The most important need for developing countries was to conceptualize their educational objectives and problems and then to choose the most cost-effective system—which could include various technologies—to achieve their goals and deal with their problems.	With the rush to introduce technology throughout and the increased number of options, the need to define educational objectives and problems before selecting technologies becomes even more important than before.
No single technology could solve all problems, and variation in learning was more dependent on how a technology was managed, organized and presented in context rather than which one was used.	This is still fundamental.

What has changed: increased flexibility and interactivity of technology; much greater choice; and much lower costs.

What hasn't changed: can't start with the technology, must start with the educational problem; costs are still a major issue; distance education works; technology can be a powerful tool for reform at the classroom level but bureaucratic inertia must be overcome, incentives changed and teachers adequately trained and motivated.

The View from the Private Sector
Needs and Opportunities

The Latin American productive sector suffers from the poor quality of labor, which in turn is the result of the chronic inadequacies of education and training. Nevertheless, there is no reason for entrepreneurs to passively watch their competitiveness erode in a world where education is increasingly important. Business should not be a silent bystander. It can act at the political scene, and it can take direct initiative. Outstanding examples of investments in education and training are to be found in business and business associations. Indeed, the business sector provides some of the most remarkable examples of the intelligent use of technology. In addition, as other papers in this book indicate, business and industry are important partners in the use of technology in education. The following comments are by

W. Bowman Cutter is Chair of the GIIC Steering Committee.

W. Bowman Cutter, of the Global Information Infrastructure Commission (GIIC.)

I predict that education in the information age will prove to be the public issue—the Rosetta Stone that lets us translate possibilities into realities. Serious exploration of this issue can help lead to a new emphasis on education as a development model.

As a public policy maker, a practitioner in the field of information, and a business decision maker, I see a variety of technology investments and technology possibilities for education in the information age. I hope to provide a sense of context, in terms of both

W. Bowman Cutter

what is driving discussions of this issue and what makes it important. I am well aware of the currents of disagreement that also flow through the discussions of this subject.

I would like to underline three points which will influence what I say. The first is that while every region of the world must necessarily find its own solution to these issues, I do believe every region can learn from what every other region has been doing. To put it more strongly, those who do not do so will only limit and cripple themselves. The second is that it is wrong to regard the private sector as simply a vendor. The private sector and the public sectors today must have a much more creative and dynamic sense of partnership, or both will fail. And finally, the U.S. does not provide the model for the world, but it does have some successes worth looking at.

RAPID CHANGE

Two major changes are creating vast economic change across the entire world, in different ways but with striking parallels. One is political and one is technological. The political change is the twin move, almost everywhere, from closed to more open competitive economies and from state-dominated to market structures. This is occurring in the dramatic moves from communism that we saw in the late 1980s and early 1990s and in the thousand smaller changes: NAFTA, Mercosur in our hemisphere, and so on. This process is occurring globally. But it is the technological changes and the rise of information technology that are even more powerful. All three fundamental basics of information technology—memory, computation, and transmission—are now changing at rates of more than 25 percent per year. For example, the microchip doubles in power almost every 18 months. Using memory per capita as a measure of economy in the way we used to use energy consumption per capita shows an increase of 65 percent per year.

Let's compare these changes to something we know about. Between 1800 and 1825 in Great Britain and Northern Europe, the Industrial Revolution involved a 25 percent change in the price of manufactured goods. That unprecedented change in the cost of these materials was enough to spark off the Industrial Revolution. We are now seeing comparable changes of roughly 25 percent per year in the principal elements of our economy. In practical terms, this means that one million computations that cost one million dollars in 1975 now cost about $45. Prices of phone calls have dropped about tenfold over the same period, and the Internet will drop these costs even further—toward a marginal cost only slightly over zero. It stands to reason that with costs like that, people in business will make more phone calls and do more computations. Today's lap-top computer is seven times faster and 1/300th of the cost of an IBM mainframe in 1975.

These changes are global. They are happening everywhere, and to be honest, people like me are forcing them to happen everywhere. Investment proposals—for example, the Mercosur region where I focus—have increased by ten times in the last year. Change of this magnitude calls for a sense of urgency from us.

NEW ROLES, NEW ALLIANCES

What is important about these changes is not an abstract interest in the rate of changes themselves but how, how much, and how fast they are changing the economies and societies in which we live. First, they are altering the structure and shape of companies and markets. Companies are becoming smaller, more focused and faster moving, and markets are vastly more competitive. Companies are deciding everywhere that if they cannot be the best at something, then someone else should do it.

Second, these changes are altering the nervous system or the infrastructure of the entire economy. We have all seen the rise of the network economy and electronic commerce. Just as with education, companies carry out more and more of their activities over the network. For example, e-mail in the U.S. now exceeds physically delivered mail. Third, these same changes are creating a much more integrated world economy. This world economy is moving far too rapidly for trade regulation and internal regulatory change to keep up with. This means isolation is no longer possible, and everyone is in competition with everyone else. Of course the flip side, and a more hopeful side, to that is that everyone also can be in alliance with everyone else.

I have a proposal on my desk to fund ventures which seek to manage telephone networks in Siberia, Russia, from Omaha, Nebraska. I have other proposals for electronic alliances between companies on different continents that will never see each other. Trade is growing twice as fast as our nations' basic economies are growing. By 2020, over 60 percent of world output will be traded. There is virtually no cost or barrier to distance competition if the product is engineering designs or financial transactions or similar kinds of intellectual endeavors. Investment capital flows inexorably to the best ideas, the best people, and the best environments.

All of this changes the role of the State and the private sector. As investment needs increase and public investment funds have become scarcer, the private sector and its funding and investment capacity have become vastly more important. So public flows of investment have remained essentially constant since 1983, whereas private investment flows have increased by 15 percent per year over the same period.

To summarize, more and more of the world output and investment is becoming international, competitive, and market-oriented. This is the environment in which, and for which, education is conducted. I want to conclude by emphasizing four points. First, we are facing a tidal wave of change. Second, this is resulting in fundamental changes in our economies. Third, these changes in turn pose new requirements and new urgencies in order for these economies to remain competitive. And finally, these new requirements come together in my view to create a new development model.

Beyond these points, I hope I have created a sense of urgency and a sense of enormous possibility. What is needed most is a sense of vision. And the private sector is a natural and willing partner in realizing that vision.

Section 2

The Unfinished Agenda: Computers in Academic Schools

The computers that will be the pivotal force for change will be those outside the control of schools and outside the schools' tendency to force new ideas into old ways.
(Seymour Papert)

■ There are good reasons to choose the easiest possible uses of computers at the early stages, and there are even stronger reasons to pursue relentlessly a policy of upgrading these uses as more experience is acquired.
(Claudio de Moura Castro)

■ Throughout the world, many schools will be engaged in the search for new, and the replacement of old, approaches. From this perspective the world can be conceived as a huge laboratory in which many small scale experiments in authentic situations will take place in order to determine which approaches for educational reform toward the future information society are successful, and under what conditions.
(W.J. Pelgrum)

[The Chilean program's] greatest strength has been its recognition that a significant impact on education by using computer technology will only be possible if teachers are capable of integrating it adequately into academic life. [Its] greatest weakness is that the teachers do not have enough time during their work day to adequately familiarize themselves with the educational potential of these instruments.
(Pedro Hepp)

The present day movement for change has an army of agents. The ultimate pressure for change will be child power.
(Seymour Papert)

A fter 20 years of earnest attempts, the hope that the computer would revolutionize academic schools remains largely unfulfilled. While there are many successful examples of the use of computers in conventional classrooms, the massive utilization that many expected still has not materialized.

Many controlled experiments show the boundless potential of computers and related technologies to enrich education. Developments in cognitive theory give the requisite conceptual explanations and justifications for these experimental uses of computers. Whether they are used in their most pedestrian forms, such as drill and practice and tutorial courseware, or under constructivist approaches, serving as tools to extend students' capabilities to explore the world and experiment, there are solid pieces of research showing strong results.

The barriers to the large scale introduction of computers are not technical but sociological or organizational. When computers are brought to existing schools, they confront conservative institutions with entrenched routines which are very difficult to break. The results are a pale image of the promises suggested by controlled experiments. Schools may refuse to use computers except under the most watered-down versions, because they are bogged down by an ethos of rigid rules, teaching habits and incentives.

The normal and predictable problems of maintenance and updating of equipment and software can be expected. But the tasks of training teachers and adjusting the schools to utilize the computer are the ones which require a long time, a clear blueprint and strong leadership. This is where all attention should focus and where success has been modest. The situation is made more difficult by the lack of consensus on how to use computers in learning. Much energy goes to defend one's school of thought against competing visions.

After a ten year experiment, Apple Computer has learned valuable and sobering lessons on how to make computers more productive in classrooms. The small box summarizing a presentation by an Apple representative illustrates some of the lessons learned.

The next paper presents the experiences of two nations. Frederick Litto has several years of experience operating Escola do Futuro from the University of São Paulo. **"Lessons from São Paulo"** offers some of what he learned producing educational software and linking Brazilian schools with those in other countries. In **"Lessons from Israel,"** Elad Peled reflects on his experience introducing computers in Israeli schools and shares some of the conclusions learned from experimental schools established in Israel.

Seymour Papert's contributions to the seminar echoed the views he expressed in **"Agents of Change."** To him, providing a little bit of computer time is like giving students a pencil for a short period per week: It cannot do much good. In contrast, there are radical ways of urging children to explore the world and solve problems with the use of permanently available computers. This would bring a revolution in education. However, schools are reluctant to embark on this bold approach and instead invent trivial pursuits with computers which are only available for limited amounts of time. Computers are thus tamed by the logic of the schools, and so are the results.

In **"How to Avoid Past Errors,"** Claudio de Moura Castro proposes an adaptive strategy for bringing computers to schools in national programs. The dilemma faced by administrators is that the more promising uses of computers take too long to implement and the political costs of idle computers and slow starts are too high to afford. Hence, the most expedient procedure is to start with simple uses that are easy on the teachers and require less organizational disruption, progressively moving to more difficult but more rewarding learning strategies. The risks faced by decision-makers are either to embark on strategies which have greater potential but take forever to be implemented, or to start with more pedestrian uses and fail to climb to higher order modes of utilization.

W. Pelgrum reflects on the European experience in computer use in **"Toward a New Educational Culture."** He offers interesting data to show how, after several years, computers remain peripheral to school education. Students hardly use them in the most critical steps of their education, mathematics and writing. According to him, this outcome is the result not of conservative teachers but of a vicious circle in which society (and in particular, parents) have expectations and attitudes which go against the grain of a more in-depth use of computers. Unless society changes its perceptions and expectations, schools will not change their ways with computers.

Pedro Hepp reviews the Chilean experience with computers in schools in **"Chilean Experiences in Computer Education Systems."** He describes the program called Enlaces and discusses the positive results as well as the difficulties encountered along the way.

Finally, in his review of **Computers in Secondary Education in Costa Rica,** Laurence Wolff concludes that, while the program is well designed and managed, the long-term payoff is still uncertain.

Lessons from Apple Computer

Kids can't wait

Steve Jobs

- At least 30 percent of budgets need to be allocated to train teachers.

- It is necessary to strike a balance between instruction and construction.

- School day and curricula cannot remain the same if computers are going to be successfully introduced.

- Conventional tests do not capture some of the consequences of using computers—such as enthusiasm, long-run changes in cognition, persistence at tasks and attitudes.

- It is necessary to educate the community in terms of what is to be expected from computers. Resistance is not only from the teachers.

- Computers are not a panacea, but can be a catalyser.

Computers in Schools

What works and what doesn't

Frederick Litto

Lessons from São Paulo: The Escola do Futuro

1. It is an illusion to try to reach all the schools or students in the short run.

- Use project schools.

- Work with teachers who are highly motivated.

2. Build systems wherein interested students/teachers come to the information, and not vice-versa.

3. Producing didactic material using new media is difficult:

- Requires true interdisciplinary team.

- Pedagogues, writer/editors, graphic design person, audio-visual person, programmer, producer have to work together.

- Requires competence, loyalty, honesty, idealistic people.

- It is not easy to keep reasonable work pace.

4. Don't take for granted traditional partners. There are hurdles with:

- Schools of Education in universities

- Companies (credibility problem)

- State postal/telephone enterprises (ignorance of international treaties)

- Teacher unions (where are the benefits?)

- Syndicate of private school owners (marketing issues)

- Book publishers (intellectual property rights)

5. The hand-holding process is long, arduous and constant.

6. The foreign language barrier is serious and requires constant monitoring (Spanish/Portuguese, Portuguese/English)

7. Don't try to teach programming to average people.

8. Train technological coordinators.

9. Make it fun.

10. Do not succumb to the fallacy of requiring the "perfect solution."

Lessons from Israel

1. Computers, when appropriately used as a tool in the hands of a trained teacher, offer an interactive, information and representation-rich learning.

2. Under favorable conditions of use, teaching and learning in this environment enhances the development of:

- Meta-curricular, higher order learning skills

- Skilled and mindful use of a wide range of cognitively empowering technologies

- Cognitive flexibility

3. Experience shows that the introduction of computers in large education systems is fraught with difficulties and pitfalls. Success requires fulfilling the following necessary conditions:

- Long and consistent pedagogical and technological support to teachers

- The development of a schoolwide theory of practice, avoiding conflicting messages

- Good computer-based curricular software

- Use of technology across subjects and classrooms

- Adequate technology access for all students

Elad Peled

- Commitment and involvement of the school principal

- Stable political support

- Avoidance of conflicting messages across levels, subject areas, teaching, testing and assessment

4. There are two approaches to the introduction of technology into education. The one that centers on the growth of the "smart learner," mindfully introduces technology into education. The other that centers on technology, floods the mind with everything technology can offer. We need to look carefully at the two options and harvest the blessings of technology, not its evils.

5. Success depends on the mobilization of educators, parents and politicians. But the process is fraught with conflicts and trade-offs:

- Parents and politicians expect short run results.

- The introduction of computers and other such technologies require much time (almost no results in first year, 3-5 years for optimal assimilation).

- Computers require a major investment.

- There are always issues of equity and equal opportunities.

Elad Peled: Lessons from Israel

Agents of Change

I magine that writing has just been invented in Foobar, a country that has managed to develop a highly sophisticated culture of poetry, philosophy and science using entirely oral means of expression. It occurs to imaginative educators that the new technology of pencils, paper and printing could have a beneficial effect on the schools of the country. Many suggestions are made. The most radical is to provide all teachers and children with pencils, paper and books and suspend regular classes for six months while everyone learns the new art of reading and writing. The more cautious plans propose starting slowly and seeing how "pencil-learning" works on a small scale before doing anything really drastic. In the end, Foobarian politicians being what they are, a cautious plan is announced with radical fanfare. Within four years a pencil and a pad of paper will be placed in every single classroom of the country so that every child, rich or poor, will have access to the new knowledge technology. Meantime the educational

Seymour Papert

Dr. Papert is Lego Professor of Learning at Massachusetts Institute of Technology. This article appeared in the Washington Post Educational Review, October 27, 1996, and is reprinted by permission.

psychologists stand by to measure the impact of
pencils on learning.

I first used this parable in the early days of computers to warn against
basing negative conclusions about computers on observations about
what happens when computers are used in a manner analogous to that
pencil experiment. At that time I ended the story with something like:
"And not surprisingly, the Foobarians concluded that pencils do not
contribute to better learning." Subsequent events have indeed shown
my fears to be well-founded: Conclusions of a Foobarian kind have in
fact slipped into the accepted wisdom of American educators. For
example, educational experiments in which children's access to computers and to computer culture was far short of what would be needed to *learn* programming have been accepted as proof that programming computers is not an educationally valuable experience for children. But in telling the Foobar story today I would give it another,
even more insidious, ending.

In fact what I now understand that the Foobarian educators would
actually do is not reject the pencil but appropriate it by finding trivial
uses of the pencil that could be carried out within their meager
resources and that would require minimal change in their old ways of
doing things. For example they might continue their oral methods of
doing chemistry but use the pencils to keep grade sheets. Or they
might develop a course in "pencil literacy" which would include learning what pencils are made of, how to sharpen them and perhaps how
to sign one's name.

I qualify this kind of appropriation as "more insidious" than merely drawing misleading conclusions because its retarding effect on
future developments is cast in the concrete of a culture, including a
profession of specialists who see their (often tenured!) jobs as implementing schools' construct of "pencilling" or, to come back to the lit-
eral plane, of "computing." And I have devoted a third of this little
essay to leading up to the point because I see it as the critical issue that
must be understood if one wants to make sense of the situation of
computers in schools and to participate in steering its future in a constructive direction. To make the point concrete, I devote the next third
to the story of the intellectual turnaround of "Bill," a high school-aged
youth in a summer work-study program for "youth at risk" in an economically depressed area of rural Maine.

Bill resented school and had virtually given up on learning if not on society itself. He had joined the project only because he would receive a small stipend, and during the first days made it quite clear that he would do only what was necessary to avoid being thrown out. But within two weeks he had become an enthusiastic participant, intellectually engaged and on his way to a level of technical expertise that astonished visiting experts on youth programs.

The simplest description of what happened is that Bill became hooked on computers. But what this lad was really "hooked on" was not the machine. It was something inside of himself: the excitement he had never known before of working on an intellectually challenging project that was truly his. And this was no one-night stand: The project was his for long enough for him to build a relationship with it; over six summer weeks he had time to feel ideas germinate in his head, to grow through persistence in the face of many setbacks and to enter the miniculture of a group of people with related interests.

The project he had chosen involved designing, building and testing computer controlled, motorized Lego vehicles. Doing so led him to seek out and use knowledge from a variety of domains: programming, physics, engineering design and—most unexpected for him—mathematics. But what a difference between this encounter and those he'd known in school. Here, he was acquiring knowledge for use, like learning a language by growing up in its country—an experience quite unlike learning a language in order to pass a test. Those high-tech computerized model cars are so rich in principles of mathematics (and the same goes for other domains of knowledge) that one could well think of the experience of their builders as learning math by living in mathland—a place that is to mathematics as France is to French. And the success of students like Bill in these environments shows that just as all children—and not only those who "have a head for French"—learn French if they live in France, so, too, all children learn mathematics if they meet it in a context that is more alive than the ordinary curriculum.

The differences between Bill's learning experience and what schools offer in the form of a few hours a week in a "computer lab" could fill many pages. Here I focus on just one: the computer lab fits into the structure of school by making "computer literacy" one more subject with its curriculum and its time slots while Bill's learning cut across all these structures. He had access to computers and other technologies all the time, whenever he needed them. He acquired knowledge at the time he needed it for a purpose ("just-in-time learning") and not because it happened to be a 10 o'clock on the 7th of May in his fifth grade year—or whatever the curriculum says to learn that fragment of knowledge. He worked with a community of people with diverse knowledge rather than with the homogenized, age-segregated community called a "class."

It is not surprising that people rooted in schools' concept of how learning should take place resist such restructuring. What is surprising is the logical distortion they resort to in order to persuade themselves that there are powerful objective reasons that make the transformation impossible. I conclude by showing how three of the fallacies encountered in attempting to argue with them are manufactured by schools themselves.

> *This kind of work is computer intensive. And giving every child a computer would be far too expensive.* Nonsense. Computers seem expensive because schools put them in the same budget category as pencils. The actual cost of production of a net-based computer powerful enough to support deep change in learning would certainly be less than $500 (and I believe that with a national effort we could bring it down to $200), and its expected lifetime would exceed five years. An annual cost of $100 per year is about 1.5 percent of direct expenditure on public schooling. Taking indirect costs and the social cost of educational failures into account, it is less than 1 percent.

> *Teachers will not be capable of providing the knowledge when it is needed.* Again a school-created obstacle. Allowing students of all ages to work together means that they are themselves a source of knowledge and besides having free access to networked computers provides an unlimited source of access to knowledge and helpers.

> *This kind of work is so contrary to the accepted idea of school that most teachers and parents will balk.* This appears to be a problem only because of the assumption that "the right way" will be imposed on everyone. It ceases to be a problem if one accepts the principle of diversity: Those who want to stay with the old way can do so.

In my new book, *The Connected Family*, I develop the idea that the computers that will be the pivotal force for change will be those outside the control of schools and outside the schools' tendency to force new ideas into old ways. We are already beginning to hear stories about the influence in classrooms of children whose access to home computers and to a home learning culture has given them a high level not only of computer expertise but also of sophistication in seeking knowledge and standards in what constitutes a serious intellectual project. The number of these children will grow exponentially in the next few years. Their pressure on schools will become irresistible.

It is 100 years since John Dewey began arguing for the kind of change that would move schools away from authoritarian classrooms with abstract notions to environments in which learning is achieved through experimentation, practice and exposure to the real world. I, for one, believe the computer makes Dewey's vision far more accessible epistemologically. It also makes it politically more likely to happen, for where Dewey had nothing but philosophical arguments, the present day movement for change has an army of agents. The ultimate pressure for change will be child power.

Computers in Schools
How to Avoid Past Errors

Several Latin American countries are getting ready to buy computers for their schools. At this point, this is neither a surprise nor revolutionary news. However, the path to the successful use of computers in schools is full of traps and pitfalls.

This paper discusses the challenges of bringing computers to schools. It also proposes a strategy beginning with easy applications of computers in education and progressively moving to more difficult but more rewarding modes. The bottom line is: *There are good reasons to choose the easiest possible uses of computers at the early stages, and there even stronger reasons to pursue relentlessly a policy of upgrading these uses as more experience is acquired.*

Claudio de Moura Castro

1. *It is vital to ensure that in the initial stages people are not demoralized by weak or disastrous results.* In the 1980s the French program to put one hundred thousand computes in schools was a severe disappointment, demoralizing its proponents and making subsequent efforts more arduous. Other countries had similar disasters. This experience cannot be ignored. It is imperative to avoid the known pitfalls in new experiments, described below.

2. In the past, many attempts to bring computers to schools failed due to the shortcomings of the hardware. But this is no longer the case. Computers are far more reliable, and have relatively long lives without too many troubles. Yet, they do require maintenance. It is imperative to make provision for maintenance budgets or preferably to allocate maintenance funds from the same budgets paying for the purchase of the computers. Otherwise, they become Trojan horses for

schools. Without maintenance, schools quickly become huge digital graveyards. Some American schools prefer to buy computers at a higher price but with longer maintenance contracts built in. This is because it is easier to obtain funds for the initial purchases than for the subsequent maintenance. Israelis go further and require that sales, maintenance and software be provided by the same vendor, to prevent one seller from blaming another and evading its obligations. Therefore, *computers should not be shipped to schools until the financial and logistical problems of maintaining them have been solved.*

3. Once the hardware problems became less important, the next hurdle in using computers in school is the software. There are many superb pieces of software today, even though most are less than superb and there is much room for improvement. A dearth of software is no longer the bottleneck. The question, however, is their choice. *Computers should not be shipped to schools without a minimum kit of software.* Without the provision of something to start with, schools will have another major hurdle added to the already painful process of introducing them. Expecting schools to purchase software before they become used to having computers in classrooms is not realistic and will delay their introduction, with all the problems that creates. Bringing computers to schools is controversial enough without the added accusations that the computers remain idle. Newspapers will surely call attention to schools without chalk and blackboards while others spend fortunes on computers that are never used.

4. After hardware and software, the third great hurdle in the introduction of computers in schools is teacher training. *Almost all evaluations indicate that lack of preparation of teachers is the number one difficulty.* Conversely, all successful initiatives result from a serious and well-thought-out effort to train teachers to use them.

5. *Therefore, the recipe to avoid the initial pitfalls is quite clear: (i) ensure proper maintenance, (ii) equip the computers with a minimum set of software (iii) train the teachers.*

6. In order to ensure the political survival of the initiative, it is necessary to ensure the immediate utilization of computers. Therefore, a fail-safe strategy is required. In other words, *a strategy is needed to get computers going immediately after their installation.* From a political point of view, it does not matter if the initial uses are neither brilliant nor ultra-creative. The greatest enemy at this initial stage is the tyranny of the purists—in particular, the fundamentalists who only believe in LOGO or constructivist strategies, rejecting simpler uses. If they have

the upper hand, initial utilization will be delayed, giving ammunition for those who dislike computers in schools.

7. There are at least *three schools of thought* in the utilization of computers in schools. Each has its strengths and weaknesses. The first sees the computer as a *teaching machine,* be it for spelling and simple arithmetic or for teaching the student along curricular lines (these are the tutorial applications). The second is to use the computer to *develop thinking skills* and to enrich education, deploying its potential to simulate, play and stimulate the intellect. The third is to *use the computer as a tool,* in the way that enterprises do. In this case, computers are used in school to prepare students to use computers at work. We could also mention a fourth use which is gaming, but this is not considered a serious use of computers by educators, even though students love games. Somehow, schools will have to choose amongst these uses or a combination of them. Individual schools should have the freedom to find their own solutions, although they should not be forced to make such a difficult and controversial decision before they are familiar with computers.

8. The relative merits and shortcomings of each of the alternatives in point 7 are by now well known. Above all, *it is not permissible to ignore the mistakes of the past.* The most lofty and noble use of computers is to teach how to think. Those who read Papert's *Mindstorms* or saw a demonstration of LOGO have had a chance to glimpse the potential of computers to develop intellectual skills. Those who saw simulation programs such as Oregon Trail or Sim City might have become fascinated with the potential of simulations, the interdisciplinary explorations and the flights of imagination which are possible with high-speed computers with vast graphic capabilities. This is the most thrilling path from an intellectual perspective. Anybody concerned with quality education will not be untouched by the potential offered by those wonderful programs. And this is where the danger lies. The accumulated experience in the last fifteen years shows the difficulties of successful implementation of these alternatives. *The development of intellectual skills does not offer a viable rationale for the massive introduction of computers in the short run.* National programs to introduce computers are well advised not to start along these lines. It will not work. It requires a long period of preparation of teachers. Trying to start along these lines is a sure recipe for failure because the public expectation is for immediate action. This is not to say that this alternative should be abandoned altogether. In fact, it may be a common goal for all in the long run and it should start immediately in some special

programs, where conditions are from the start more favorable. These should be islands of experimentation and creativity. They depend on intellectual leadership on the part of some teachers. But this is not the way to start on the massive scale which is required by national programs.

9. *The most pedestrian and unremarkable use of computers is to drill students in arithmetic operations, solving equations, correcting spelling and so on. But in actual fact, this is what has really worked in schools.* The reason is simple. Teachers are the ultimate arbiters of whether the computers are used or kept idle. If they do not want to use them, academic schools are unable to force them. Preventing the boycotting of computers in the classrooms is virtually impossible. And unless computers help rather than hinder, they will remain turned off. *Teachers will only use the computer if they find that it benefits them.* Teachers simply will not use them if it takes too long to master the skills of using the machine and its software, if it takes longer to prepare classes, if there is the risk of an embarrassing situation where the computer gets stuck or crashes (with the even greater risk that some insolent kid will get it unstuck), if its proposed use does not follow the curriculum, if the skills learned are not required in tests. Any of these situations will kill the use of computers. But experience shows that *teachers appreciate the infinite patience of computers* to drill again and again in multiplication or division or any other repetitive task. In addition, kids prefer doing these computations on the screen rather than with paper and pencil. These are the uses that please teachers. The reasons could not be more down to earth, but drill and practice programs save time, energy and drudgery, and hence they are used. As an initial strategy for primary school, there are excellent reasons not to snub this use of computers. On the contrary, it is necessary to provide schools with drill and practice programs and to prepare teachers to use them. It is likewise necessary to sell this strategy intelligently, lest it acquire a negative connotation.

10. Along this line, some additional thoughts are in order. *Gone are the days when it made sense to write drill and practice programs in Basic,* in order to teach irregular verbs or to recall historical dates. Gone are the days in which authoring tools were offered to teachers in the hopes that they would translate their courses into tutorial programs. The big software houses killed the hopes for such amateurish approaches. Today, a run-of-the-mill educational software program will cost at least $100,000 and the more sophisticated a lot more. Therefore, national programs to introduce computers need to check existing software and

decide whether there are exceptional cases where a new software needs to be commissioned.

11. *Teaching students how to use computers as a productive tool is a safe way to bring computers to schools.* If there are some applications which most enterprises use, it makes sense to teach students how to work with the most versatile of all tools existing at the end of the century. This is a constructive use of computers in schools and an easy path to embark on. In concrete terms, it means teaching students how to use a word processor (desk-top publishing is the next step), a spreadsheet, a data base and graphic tools. There is ample legitimacy for such uses and the software is immediately available. In addition, considering the widespread availability of computer courses teaching these skills, there is usually a good supply of instructors. *Computers should not be shipped to schools without a complete package of productivity software.* (If costs are a consideration here, there are many inexpensive ersatz to the standard Microsoft and Novell packages.) Installing the software is a task beyond the capabilities of schools. The next task is to develop appropriate strategies to use these productivity tools. To begin with, touch typing is a most valuable skill. Keyboard training is good way to start, even though not all proponents of computers in school share this view. *It is also important to prepare teachers to give their students interesting and practical exercises for the productivity tools.* We should not expect the teachers to invent creative examples or to develop templates that are interesting to the students. These examples should be close to the world of the students and, if possible, useful to them. Sorting data in data bases can be a good exercise in Boolean logic, but to do this teachers need good data banks to use with their students. If a teacher or a group of students are willing to construct a data base of Formula One championships, great. This is an excellent exercise. But a fail-safe strategy is required. Good data must be available—perhaps on past presidents, production statistics, soccer championships. By the same token, practical uses of spreadsheets should be available (for instance, personal finances, used car prices, costing of a school party).

12. To minimize the risk of having computers sit idle, *it may be a good idea to allow students to play freely with them.* There is evidence that even games which do not claim any educational consequences can bring some learning. In addition, there are many games which do have considerable potential for developing important cognitive skills. Playing with computers is in itself a learning of consequence. Certainly, public officials could never admit it, but hacking and

pirating software is an intellectual pursuit that is not entirely without learning outcomes.

To sum up, it seems reasonable to require that schools receiving computers should be required to make them available to students a number of hours outside class time. Even though distribution of users is highly skewed, this is better than denying access to all.

Toward a New Educational Culture

Possibilities and Challenges For a Reform of Learning in Europe

W·J· Pelgrum

A s a result of a number of developments (such as the upcoming year 2000 and recent innovations in communication and information technologies or CIT), there has been increasing societal and political awareness that a transition from industrial to information societies is underway. The belief is growing that this transition will lead to profound changes in the curriculum and organization of the educational system that may be as extensive as those that took place when societies changed from agricultural to industrial. Vivid discussions are currently taking place at national and European levels about the desired direction of these changes. The general expectation is that it will be necessary to induce skills for life-long learning, and associated with

Dr. Pelgrum is senior researcher and program leader at the Center for Applied Educational Research at the University of Twente in the Netherlands. This paper was originally presented at a February 1997 European Commission Workshop in Luxembourg.

this that instead of focusing on teacher centered ways of transfer of information (the reproductive model), more student centered ways for acquiring information (the productive mode) will be necessary. The instructional paradigm for realizing the latter mode is Socratic dialogue.

From a long research tradition on educational reforms we may conclude that changes will not occur if the intended innovations are not seen as useful and practical by teachers. Hence, it is very important to have seminars in which, at an early stage of thinking about the restructuring of education, there is an opportunity to communicate from the teacher's point of view about the directions for change and the recommended procedures for reshaping education's future. This paper addresses the following questions:

1. What have we learned from the past about the intended objectives, successes and failures of educational innovations in the area of information technologies?

2. What are the main proposed directions for the intended changes, and what are the dilemmas which should be solved?

3. To what extent is there already sufficient awareness of the need for change? What is known about the current situation in schools with regard to the adoption of CIT-based learning? Results from recent surveys will be shown to provide an estimate of the current situation.

4. Which systems for navigating the education mammoth tanker to a promising future can we at this moment envisage, and what should be the role of different groups of stakeholders in education during this process?

PREVIOUS INNOVATIONS IN INFORMATION TECHNOLOGY

It is reasonable to expect that the future reform of education will rely very heavily on further development and application of information and communication technologies. Before taking a look at the road ahead, it may be illuminating to first look over our shoulder to see how our journey along the road of introducing information technologies in education has gone so far. Therefore a short historical sketch of information technology in education follows, moving from the euphoria of the 1980s via the disappointment of the early 1990s to the current revived euphoria. Finally, the question of the extent to which our past experiences can guide our way to the future will be examined.

THE 1980S, WHEN THE INTRODUCTION OF INFORMATION TECHNOLOGY IN EDUCATION BEGAN

In the early 1980s, microcomputers became available for mass production and were purchased in great numbers for office purposes. The general expectation in many countries was that this technology would completely change society and education, and that quick responses would be needed in order to prepare the citizens of the future. As a consequence governments (e.g., France and the United Kingdom) started big campaigns, accompanied and sometimes preceded by private initiatives, to provide computers to schools and to organize teacher training. The expectation was that these tools not only would be important for preparing students to function in an information society, but also would have very beneficial effects on the instructional process and outcomes of education. From survey results it can be seen that by 1985, in many countries, already most upper secondary schools had access to microcomputers, and by the late 1980s for lower secondary schools. Primary schools were usually the last to be equipped. Nowadays, in most E.U. countries all secondary schools have access to computers. In primary schools this is not yet the case in all countries.

Surveys also showed that computers were mainly used as an add-on to the existing school curriculum (that is, to teach students how to handle hardware and software), rather than a modern tool for instruction. Many analyses were conducted to find the possible causes of the stagnating integration of computers in the curriculum of schools. The main factors convincingly shown to play a role were lack of adequate preparation of teachers, lack of time to get acquainted with this new technology, and lack of software.

These findings were in line with the expectations of skeptics who in the 1980s argued that a fundamental change of education as a result of introducing computers could not be expected, because so many things have to change at the same time (curriculum materials, instructional strategies, class management, the role of the teacher, the organization of the school, etc.).

THE EARLY 1990S: DISAPPOINTMENT

The many investigations on the effects of the infusion of computers on changing the curriculum of schools clearly resulted in disappointment at the political level. There were many signs throughout Europe that governments were inclined to give up their huge investments in these developments. Also, at the school level, there were indications that further reform was not expected. It was illustrative, for example, that many Dutch school principals expected in the early 1990s that no further changes would be needed. It looked as though people had accepted the then-prevailing situation and were just intending to continue the use of computers in education as an add-on: in elementary education mainly as a tool for drill and practice, and in secondary education as an object, with only marginal use for instruction. Such uses would not require huge investments of additional equipment or any radical changes in the teaching-learning process.

From statistics collected in 1995, one may conclude that the integrative use of computers was still very low. For instance, when students were asked how often they used computers in mathematics lessons, only a minority indicated that this was frequently the case.

The conclusion seems warranted that two years ago computer use for mathematics instruction was still a marginal phenomenon and that this situation is not much different from what was found in 1992.

To summarize: developments in the 1980s were strongly technologically driven and often based on the naïve expectation that simply introducing new technologies in education would result in fundamental changes. Arguably, there was a particular lack of clearly-articulated educational objectives for desired changes.

THE LATE 1990S: A REVIVED INTEREST IN INFORMATION AND COMMUNICATION TECHNOLOGIES

In just a few years' time, the situation has changed completely. Suddenly there is a massive world-wide movement of unprecedented interest in information technologies. Again the expectations about the possibilities of this technology are very high. One might wonder whether current expectations are more realistic than comparable ones in the early 1980s. There are several reasons to argue that they are:

1. The increased technological possibilities, especially for communication purposes. (The change of standard vocabulary, namely from IT to CIT [or ICT], illustrates this phenomenon.)

2. The increased access to information via the World Wide Web.

The Internet has greatly improved the societal acceptance of information technologies.

3. Societal momentum. Where in the past most access to communication possibilities took place at offices, suddenly many citizens have access. Also, the access to information has improved. With instantaneous access to databases all over the world, one need not rely on databases that are available only locally.

As a result of this technological development, several governments throughout Europe intend to equip all schools with the facilities for access to communication networks such as Internet. Does this mean that education is again confronted with technology-driven change? Is this merely new "hype" with a short life expectancy? Is it old wine in new barrels? Will it again result in disappointment in a couple of years? There are no direct answers to these questions, but it is arguable that this could indeed occur if the developments are not be embedded in a good pedagogical rationale.

With regard to the last point, there is some reason for hope. Unlike the situation in the 1980s, a much more pronounced educational rationale seems to be gaining momentum at the higher political levels while simultaneously gaining increasing social acceptance. In the next section we will examine some of the main lines of thinking with regard to this new rationale.

TOWARD NEW EDUCATIONAL OBJECTIVES: THE MAIN DIRECTIONS PROPOSED FOR THE INTENDED CHANGES, AND THE DILEMMAS WHICH MUST BE SOLVED

When we analyze documents in circulation offering perspectives on the future (e.g., in the E.U. and at the level of national governments), we can distill a number of expectations or beliefs about the desirable directions for educational change. They can be roughly summarized as follows:

As a result of the rapid technological developments, we are in a process of change from industrial to information societies. Just as education needed to be adapted when societies changed from agricultural to industrial, an educational change of analogous or even greater magnitude is needed in order to educate the citizens of the future. In comparison with the great stability of life in agricultural societies and the increased level of societal change during the industrialization period, societal change processes will be in an even higher gear in the future. Education must change in order to adequately prepare the citizens of the future to function in a society in a constant state of flux. Therefore, the current educational paradigm—mass production of ready-made knowledgeable citizens with certificates which qualify them for a long-lasting career—must be replaced by educational models which qualify citizens in terms of life-long learning skills for a society in which CIT is one of the main infrastructure pillars.

What are the educational consequences of this societal philosophy? Without trying to be exhaustive, I will just cite in the following table (Table 1) a number of potential consequences which are often encountered in various documents.

It is apparent from the table that most dreams about educational changes can be described almost without reference to CIT. Therefore the question is, what does CIT have to do with this? The answer is

Table 1. A new educational model.

Actor	Current Situation	Future
School	• Isolated from society • Most information on school functioning secret	• Integrated in society • Information openly available
Teacher	• Initiator of instruction • Whole-class teaching • Evaluates student • Low emphasis on communcation skills	• Help students to find appropriate instructional path • Independent learning • Helps student to evaluate progress • High emphasis on communcation skills
Student	• Passive • Learns most at school • Little teamwork • Takes questions from books • Learns answer to questions • Low interest in learning	• Active • Learning at school and outside school • Much teamwork • Asks questions • Finds answers to questions • High interest
Parent	• Hardly active in learning process • No steering of instruction • No life-long learning model	• Very active • Co-steering • Parents provide model

that many of these changes can only be implemented with the help of CIT. Some may challenge this reasoning by saying that many of these ideas already have been implemented in progressive and innovative schools—the ones based on the philosophies of Freinet, Montessori, and Steiner, for example—and these could offer good models for the future of education. The last part of the statement is open to dispute, and many practitioners from traditional schools would be inclined to argue that a substantial number of children would not be able to survive in such open educational settings.

If we admit that the objectives of progressive schools cannot be realized in the education system at large, how can we be confident that such reform is possible using CIT? A related question is how an awareness of the need for change in society at large can be raised. This brings us to the next question, concerning the current awareness of the need for change.

CURRENT AWARENESS OF THE NEED FOR CHANGE

Irrespective of how rational, plausible and relevant the new objectives for education may sound, we must be realistic in our expectations about the extent to which these ideals are shared by a large group of people. It is very promising to see that, unlike the situation in the early 1980s, there is now much more pronounced policy-making in Europe with regard to a reform of educational objectives, even at the E.U. level. However, far more information will be needed before a large mass of educational practitioners can be convinced that something worthwhile is on the way.

In terms of our main challenges, who is currently aware that our knowledge is (or, more importantly, will be) quickly outdated? How could we know? What tools do we have to determine where we are and what realistic intermediate objectives to strive for? How will we know if education is able to induce life-long learning skills? How can these skills be defined? Why should teachers give up lecturing to whole classes if in many cases they believe that is the most efficient way to transfer information? Who will show us what is wrong if we do it this way rather than another way? Should education be equipped with the navigation tools for guiding the trip to the future?

Clearly, another educational culture is needed—for instance, one in which educational partners get very worried if they see statistics showing that many students say they dislike mathematics a lot—certainly not a good basic attitude for life-long learning. Or maybe in the future, countries will be very upset if whole-class teaching is still so popular with teachers.

Citizens' increased awareness of their knowledge and skills will be very important for a change of culture, and low-threshold tools should probably be made available to increase this awareness. Such tools might be derived from current popular tools which elicit curiosity, such as the self-assessment quizzes that are frequently included in popular periodicals. If they are scientifically guided (based on reliable and valid instruments) and seriously answered, such tools may be low-threshold and attractive ways to make people aware of the possibilities for self-assessment and self-guided learning, given the availability of tele-learning opportunities. Especially if such efforts are directed at the skills for life-long learning— teamwork, job knowledge, and so on— they could well fit within the current global frameworks.

NAVIGATION INTO THE FUTURE OF EDUCATION

The above sections have posed many questions that illustrate challenges to potential future reforms in education. The major dilemma confronting us is that we must shape the future without knowing how it will look.

Brummelhuis and Rapmund (1996) have succinctly articulated the challenge facing us:

It is likely that the information society will resemble the industrial society in only a few aspects. It will use other definitions, also for education. From this perspective our current education can be characterized as industrial heritage. If the industrial society vanishes, also the associated definition of education will disappear. This implies that education of the future is not a product which self-evidently is built upon our current education, but could be something new, which will arise from a new societal concept. Consequently, education of the future is not a design problem, but rather a participation problem......In other words: the future will define its own 'education'.
(translation WJP)

What is the way out of the dilemma of participating in an enterprise which has an unpredictable end? Maybe an analogy will help.

As there are no blueprints for a future society, educational reform toward creating the education of the future cannot be designed but is rather a discovery tour of participation in innovative approaches embedded in a process of successive approximation, characterized by :

- Sensitivity to societal developments and timely responses

- Awareness of the capacity for change of students, parents, teachers, and schools

- An adequate system for information provision on what works and what doesn't.

Taking into account the many different factors which play a role in educational reform processes and the impossibility of changing isolated aspects of an education system, the reshaping of education should be based on multidisciplinary approaches in which technical know-how, implementation expertise, training facilities, scientific evaluation and an orientation to practical feasibility are closely interwoven.

If we accept the metaphor of a voyage of discovery, we need the voyagers to take the risks. In a lot of cases they will not reach the promised land. However, the ones who reach it will show the videos back home, and many will follow their travels to that land.

One problem with this metaphor is that whole groups of students need to accompany the voyager: how can we minimize the risk that something will happen, that they will be damaged? Maybe some guidelines could be created, with one of the criteria being that the experience in itself (the journey) should be healthy enough even if the intended goal is not reached. However, if we want to avoid pedagogical paternalism, who is going to determine if this is the case?

Maybe here the pragmatic metaphor of the market place would be applicable: If there are enough interested buyers, there is a market. But where then is the place? Here the answer might be that these places will need to be developed: educational market places (virtual and real) where people can orient themselves about products and prices (material as well as immaterial). Especially if (educational) experts and (educational) consumer organizations can monitor the quality of these products, a relatively safe climate for educational reform might be created. The European award scheme for high-quality multimedia products might be a good way to find the good examples which may be exhibited in such a market place.

Given that the future of our societies and hence of education cannot be predicted, active participation in exploring the possibilities and an approach of *successive approximation* is needed. This term, which stems from learning psychology, illustrates very well the main features of the proposed approach: proceed in small steps, using feedback to keep the good and throw away the bad. The main implication of the focus on participation rather than designing from blueprints is that the viability of new approaches is determined on the basis of positive or negative feedback from educational practice. This places the students and teachers in the center of the new developments. In such a scenario it will be vital to install a good system for information on the progress being made. Therefore it will be necessary to develop adequate means of informing all educational partners about the direction in which education is moving.

Another important question with regard to shaping the future of education is at which age to start. It may be argued that new models of learning and instruction require a completely new behavioral repertoire from future students and of their immediate environment. It involves preparing children at a young age to integrate the use of information technology as tools in their lives. This is not usually a problem for young children; rather, it is the parents who will need to change. This will be a slow process, but could be accelerated by simultaneously caring for the current practices and having courage to undertake experiments. The concept of tele-playing might be explored: offering parents (and even grandparents who frequently interact with their grandchildren) opportunities for "self-assessment" of their children and offering them examples of how via games the social, emotional, motor, and cognitive development of the child may be stimulated. Such programs (which can be made accessible via Internet-TV) not only stimulate the child, but also bring citizens who grew up in a CIT-poor environment in touch with advances in this area. This is not too far distant from what happens now in TV programs for young children (e.g., "Sesame Street").

NEW ROLES FOR EDUCATIONAL STAKEHOLDERS

All of the above implies that the current roles of educational stakeholders need to change. A new interaction will need to exist between educational practitioners and domain and CIT experts in the evaluation of emergent practices, with interaction among all the stakeholders.

SUMMARY AND CONCLUSIONS

The notion that worldwide, our societies are in the midst of drastic change is currently very popular politically at both international and national levels, and shared by an unknown number of citizens. The reasoning behind this belief and its potential implications for guiding processes of educational reform can be roughly characterized as follows.

1. As a result of the rapid technological developments, industrial production is and will be increasingly automated. Analogous to the way that industrial production activities replaced manual labor when societies changed from agricultural to industrial, it is believed that in the future many human professional activities will be focused on handling information. In comparison with the increased level of societal change during the industrialization period, replacing the stability of life in agricultural societies, it is expected that societal change processes will be even in a higher gear in the future. Consequently citizens will need to be constantly aware of these changes and able to adapt to them.

2. Education must change in order to adequately prepare the citizens of the future to function in a society in a constant state of flux. Consequently, the current educational paradigm of mass production of ready-made knowledgeable citizens with certificates which qualify them for a long-lasting job career must be replaced by educational models which qualify citizens in terms of life-long learning skills in a society in which CIT is one of the main infrastructural pillars.

3. As there are no blueprints of a future society, educational reform cannot be designed but is a rather a matter of participation in innovative approaches embedded in a process of successive approximation, characterized by :

● Sensitivity to societal developments and timely responses

● Awareness of the capacity for change of students, parents, teachers, and schools

● An adequate system for information about what works and what doesn't

4. Taking into account the many factors which play a role in educational reform processes and the impossibility of changing isolated aspects of an education system, the reshaping of education should be based on multidisciplinary approaches that weave together technical

know-how, implementation expertise, training facilities, scientific evaluation, and an orientation to practical feasibility.

An important implication from the previous point is that throughout the world many schools will be engaged in the search for new, and the replacement of old, approaches. From this perspective the world can be conceived as a huge laboratory in which many small scale experiments in authentic situations will take place in order to determine which approaches for educational reform toward the future information society are successful, and under what conditions.

Chilean Experiences in Computer Education Systems

Pedro Hepp

During the current decade, Chile has undergone extensive reform at all levels of its educational system. For the first time in the country's history, all the necessary ingredients have come together in the monumental task of turning reform into a reality extending to the classrooms of every school, improving the fairness and quality of the nation's entire educational system. Indeed, Chile can show that during this entire decade it has benefited from political decisiveness, budgetary support and a national consensus as well as the ability to propose, articulate and implement proposals for coherent change in its educational system.

Chile's educational reform covers a broad spectrum of initiatives: a gradual but significant increase in teacher salaries, improvements in school infrastructure, new textbooks and modern educational

Dr. Hepp is National Links Network Coordinator of the Universidad de La Frontera.

resources, a new curriculum, and new plans and programs for basic and intermediate education. At the same time, a review of teaching and learning methodologies has been carried out at all levels of education, with a view to developing a teaching system that is more efficient, more attractive and more relevant to the lives of students.

Educational reform goes hand in hand with numerous other changes in Chilean society. Chile currently has an open and internationally competitive economy, and it has modernized its social security system as well as various state services such as the civil registry and internal taxes. Banking and trade have also changed and modernized their services and competitiveness, as has a portion of the health system. A modernization of the judicial branch is now pending, although it is currently only in the planning stage. Chile is viewed as a country that is actively progressing toward a modern, globally integrated society, adding value to its products and higher quality to the lives of its citizens.

This broad modernizing effort is due in part to the initiatives of the Chilean Ministry of Education to provide students and teachers with modern instruments for handling and accessing the emerging and rapidly growing digital world. To this end, by the end of the century every secondary school and at least half of all elementary schools will have access to computer technology and communications networks. This initiative is known as the Links Network (La Red Enlaces) and its major achievements and difficulties are described below.

ACHIEVEMENTS AND DIFFICULTIES INVOLVING COMPUTER EDUCATION SYSTEMS
Chilean educational reform

In general and from the perspective of the Links Network, several factors of Chilean reform have contributed to its success.

The first is the stability of the government's education-related policies. The Chilean reform began in early 1990, and has kept a coherent message, continuity in its major lines and stable teams of individals in its leadership positions for almost a decade through two governments and five ministries of education.

Second, this very stability has allowed the educational system to gain experience and to deepen successful initiatives and change those which, over time, have required adjustment. The major processes relating to administration of the reform (public bids, wide-scale training, the creation of stable work groups, etc.) have led to gradual improvement thanks to the high technical capacity and growing experience of those leading the reform, and despite the bureaucratic tradition of the state apparatus.

Third, the Ministry of Education has been able to support reform through a sustained increase in monetary resources. Thus, for 1998 the sector's budget exceeds historic funding levels, for the most part maintaining current policies while providing for an increase in school subsidies and higher teacher salaries.

Finally, the Ministry of Education has been able to involve experts from across the entire political spectrum in reform-related work and keep close ties with the teachers, significantly increasing their salaries and improving their work environments. It also has begun to activate the schools of education in the university system, helping them update their methods and raise the level of the teaching profession.

Thus, the stability of reform over time, the extent and consistency of the proposals, and leadership at a high technical level have allowed the Chilean educational system to effectively take educational reform into practice in the classroom.

Among the factors that have made progress on the reform difficult, the most notable is the need to give teachers more time to assimilate changes in their educational practices. Other difficulties include the lack of leadership among the administrative teams in many educational establishments, the difficulty of assimilating changes among various sectors of society (particularly parents, guardians and business groups), and finally, the need for the Ministry of Education itself, at the national level, to adapt its activities to the rate of change that is expected of the teachers.

THE LINKS NETWORK

The Links Network for computer education is a component of the Chilean Ministry of Education's MECE Program for improving quality and fairness. The mission of Links is to integrate computer and network technologies as teaching and learning resources in the Chilean education system. In 1997, 1,500 educational establishments formed part of this initiative, and the network will cover half of all elementary schools and all high schools (intermediate education) by the year 2000. Chile has approximately 10,000 educational establishments, 130,000 teachers and close to 2,800,000 students.

From the beginning, Links has centered its proposal around the following assumption: Computer systems and networks are new instruments for *all* teachers and students, with roles in educational, administrative, professional and social activities. The use of these technologies and the possibilities they represent in an academic establishment is a gradual process mediated by the culture of the establishment and the leadership capacity of its management team.

Educational establishments that join the Links Network obtain computer and network equipment, educational software, free connectivity to e-mail (Internet) and two years of training and technical assistance for a maximum of twenty teachers. The quantity of equipment received by each establishment depends on the number of students, as described below.

A summary of the greatest strength and weakness of Links places them in counterpoint. *Links' greatest strength has been its recognition that a significant impact on education by using computer technology will only be possible if teachers are capable of integrating it adequately into academic life. Links' greatest weakness is that the teachers do not have enough time during their work day to adequately familiarize themselves with the educational potential of these instruments.*

Support components

Links has the following support components to assist it in meeting its objectives. The advantages and disadvantages of each will be discussed:

University technical assistance network

The Ministry of Education has the support of over twenty universities throughout the country, which design and carry out teacher training. Each university develops teaching materials, work guides, its own proposals, and so on, and has a number of trainers that assist the schools on a weekly basis to develop training.

The advantage of this relationship between the Ministry of Education, the universities and the schools is that it completes a virtuous cycle which has historically been only weakly connected. These universities are in direct contact with the reforms promoted by the Ministry of Education; they participate in designing proposals and are the first to be informed. This very fact has an immediate impact on the training of new teachers from the schools of education, since it is often the university professors themselves at these schools who participate in Links and thus remain in close contact with the reform movement.

The disadvantage of this relationship is that most universities still have relatively slow administrative procedures, high operating costs and extensive needs for resources in order to be able to appropriately carry out their work. This reduces the capacity of some universities to adapt to the pace of the reform and the requirements of Links, and they are unable to allocate additional resources to computer education systems. Some universities do understand that education is a very fertile field for research at the primary level and that Links offers a true laboratory for exploring new methodologies and teaching resources, with a positive impact on their academic activities.

The ministry of education national network

The Ministry of Education is administratively decentralized across the country's thirteen regions and throughout its provinces. For more than a year, this organization has actively participated in Links in two senses: it is connected to the same network as the schools, and its approximately eight hundred supervisors are being trained in computer education systems.

The advantage of this direct relationship between the Ministry and the schools is multiple:

- The classroom teachers see that the "educational system"—not just the classroom teachers themselves but also the ministerial employees—has also decided to use the technology. In other words, there is a validation of the technology within the educational system.

- Classroom teachers have begun to receive information directly, immediately and without administrative filters over the information super-highway from the Ministry of Education in Santiago. This has allowed the teachers to begin to appreciate the technology as a useful resource, as they receive union and institutional information. For its part, the central Ministry in Santiago is making a determined effort to offer content relevant to teachers via the Links Network.

- Various reform initiatives unrelated to computer technology have begun to use the network for their own purposes, recognizing it as a simple and powerful means of disseminating their proposals, comments or questions to a large number of teachers quickly and simultaneously. That is to say, Links is beginning to be perceived as an instrument for supporting the administration of ministerial initiatives while at the same time serving as a mechanism for monitoring them.

The disadvantage of this relationship is that the many ministerial employees who have had little opportunity to access this technology resent the speed with which the ministry is changing its practices and resist this aspect of educational modernization. Because this method of receiving and transmitting information is completely new in the Chilean educational system, "official" information is still perceived as that which arrives on sheets of paper with the proper ministerial letter-head. In addition, the suspicion persists that information on the network may be lost and that matters of a greatest importance will remain subject to regular procedures, which are lengthy and involve multiple layers of intermediate employees, rarely filtering down to the classroom teachers.

National coordination

The Links network is included as a component of the MECE Program, which is leading the reform. Links is administered partly by a dedicated and multidisciplinary team of professionals (educators, engineers and psychologists) based at the Ministry of Education in Santiago, and partly by another multidisciplinary team (educators, engineers, graphic designers, journalists and psychologists) based at the Institute for Computer Education Systems at the Universidad de La Frontera in Temuco, a city some seven hundred kilometers south of Santiago.

The advantage of splitting the national coordination tasks into two groups is that it allows one group (Santiago) to focus on the administrative processes (invitations to bid for hardware, software and Web sites, budgets, inter-ministerial coordination, agreements with universities, legal aspects, etc.) and the other group (Temuco) to focus on technological-educational aspects (content of the training sessions, policy guidelines, network administration, inter-university relationships, etc.).

It is important to note that the Institute for Computer Education Systems at the Universidad de La Frontera at Temuco is also responsible for designing and implementing the training of teachers in all schools comprising the Links Network in southern Chile, from Temuco to Antarctica. This direct contact with the schools affords the group field experience and a very realistic perspective, from which the Ministry of Education may benefit in setting its policies.

The disadvantage of this split organization is that on occasion, the distance makes it difficult for decisions relating to policies, agreements, and so on to be sufficiently discussed and developed by both groups simultaneously. A great deal of travel is necessary between the two cities for coordination and analysis meetings. Moreover, the Temuco group maintains weaker links with other reform-oriented groups based in Santiago.

A development center

The Ministry of Education has a special agreement with the Universidad de La Frontera to maintain a center for development and experimentation in computer education systems at that university's Institute for Computer Education Systems. This development center supports the national Links coordination efforts in decisions requiring technical opinions and policy guidance. Examples are the type of technology to be introduced into the schools, the type of educational software to be used, and the educational benefits of the Internet.

The advantage of having this Development Center is that the Ministry of Education has decided that the introduction of computer technology and networks to the schools requires an ongoing capacity for reflection and experimentation on a small scale before a full-scale launch. The Institute for Computer Education Systems is performing pilot experiments at the very schools in its region that have joined Links, with a view to evaluating new alternatives that have a real educational impact. Because a significant part of the teacher training for southern Chile is carried out at this same Institute, this center is well-grounded in educational realities.

The disadvantage of having only one Development Center is that not all of the country's varied educational situations are covered. It would be more appropriate to have three centers—one in the north, corresponding to the situation of the schools in the four northern regions; another in Santiago, covering the urban education situation; plus the current center in southern Chile. That structure would cover the entire Chilean educational spectrum.

Businesses

The quantitative goals of the Links Network can be achieved only through the participation of the private sector. Every year, the Ministry of Education makes a significant effort to acquire computer technology on the market and to finance teacher training, but it needs the private sector to achieve all its goals. To this end, the Ministry of Education is developing what it calls an "Open Incorporation Plan" (PIA): if a school acquires the basic hardware through company donations, the Ministry automatically incorporates this school into Links, giving it software, connectivity and most importantly teacher training through an affiliated university.

The advantage of the PIA is that schools and companies have begun to mobilize, both to obtain resources and to formalize their commitment to education. Companies have an incentive to take advantage of the donations law, through which they receive tax benefits.

The disadvantage of this initiative is that the donations law is not expeditious and appropriate for donations from businesses to groups of schools. Furthermore, businesses willing to make donations are still rare, partly because of their lack of experience in this regard and possibly also because of the lack of stronger incentives. Nevertheless, the Ministry of Education is involved in a very active campaign through the press and brochures to guide and familiarize businesses in this regard.

Use of computer and network technologies

Links was conceived as a "seed equipment" project—i.e., with enough computers per establishment that the teachers could evaluate the technology within the context of their establishment's educational plans. Through other mechanisms, such as the donations law, schools and high schools can expand their equipment. The equipment is distributed as follows:

<100 students:	3 computers, 1 printer
100-300 students:	6 computers, 2 printer
>300 students:	9 computers, 2 printer

Although the current equipment allows most teachers to familiarize themselves with the technology, in general it is still insufficient to work comfortably through a complete course, with three or four students per computer. Although this has led to the development of novel structures for the use of technology in the classroom, it continues to be problematic for adaptation and innovation.

Finally, it is necessary to address the following equipment problems:

- Maintenance and insurance. The equipment has a use-life of three to five years, depending on its use and the environment (e.g., rural schools with equipment exposed to higher levels of humidity and dust). In addressing deterioration, teachers in poor communities are rarely able to engage a maintenance service or pay for repairs.

- Installation of equipment. The cost of installing the equipment represents approximately 30 percent of the school's equipment cost. Although the operation of the equipment is conditional upon proper electrical installation and the local network, the specifications for the materials and the execution of the work must be constantly reviewed in order to mitigate these costs.

CHALLENGES

Links is greatly expanding its coverage. At the same time, computer technology is changing rapidly, work proposals are being continuously updated, and the educational potential of the Internet is growing. In this environment, Links will, and must, continue to balance implementation with experimentation.

The greatest challenges lie in expanding coverage while maintaining good quality levels in terms of teacher support; deepening this support by seeking to improve the integration of the teachers' activities with the use of technology in the classroom; developing strategies to take advantage of the Internet with its potential for communications and multimedia information; and gaining active involvement on the part of the private sector in maintaining computer labs. Finally, a significant expansion of Links in the rural sector is pending implementation, as is the contribution of Links to the national Montegrande project for advanced high schools.

An important reason for developing an attractive proposal for the private sector's participation in Links is the long-term sustainability of the computer equipment. Indeed, Links' most expensive component is hardware (approximately 70 percent of the investment), which has a use-life of approximately 5 to 7 years. Beginning in the year 2000, a higher rate of investment is needed in order to replace equipment.

Moreover, elementary schools and high schools must gradually assume the cost of connecting to the Internet, with the ever-increasing demand for bandwidth and accessibility. This will imply more lines, greater speed, better modems, larger servers and finally, higher recurring costs to establishments merely to maintain their current systems. This imminent reality and the means of addressing it will be the central part of the strategy of incentives and participation by the private sector.

Notwithstanding the potential for private sector participation, the Ministry of Education must maintain a complete support structure (hardware, software, networks, installations and assistance) for establishments prevented by poverty or isolation from participating effectively in this strategy and gaining the benefits for schools operating under isolated conditions.

RECOMMENDATIONS

Educational reform has been successful largely because of its stability over time, the presence of a broad national consensus with regard to the need to modernize education, the consistency and extent of the content and proposals for reform, the growing availability of resources, and leadership at a high technical level. As the next stage of development, the following measures are recommended:

- that training be considered as part of the teachers' work day

- that the teacher training centers be integrated into the educational reform initiatives

- that processes to incorporate computer technology throughout the administration be a priority

- that as many experimentation centers be created as there are educational situations in this country, and that attention be given to the experiences of other countries

- that measures such as the donations law and outreach through the press, meetings and brochures be pursued aggressively

- that computer equipment upgrade and maintenance policies be implemented from an early point

- that investments continue in good national communications infra-structure, as well as in expertise in engineering and education

Costa Rica
Computers in Secondary Education

T he Computers in Secondary Education program in Costa Rica is part of a broader strategy articulated by the President of Costa Rica to make his country a leader in technology. The recent announcement by INTEL

Laurence Wolff

that it will build a $300 million micro-processor plant in Costa Rica, which will generate 3,500 jobs as well as billions of dollars in future export revenues, is one result of this strategy.

THE PROGRAM

The program seeks to (a) contribute to the development of logical thinking and creativity; (b) improve learning in specific disciplines; and (c) encourage more positive attitudes towards science and technology, greater self esteem and increased technology competency ("fluidez tecnologica"). The approach is strongly influenced by "constructivist" pedagogy, explained in a Costa Rican document as follows: "Learning is greater when students are involved in the construction of a significant product. This involves construction of things in the external world and simultaneous construction in the mind's interior." Under this approach the computer is used to encourage student-initiated inquiry. Only interested and committed teachers are asked to participate. Communities pay for maintenance through charging for services provided outside school hours. A parallel program in primary education has been underway for some time, especially utilizing LOGO to develop logical thinking.

There are now 26 computer laboratories in 20 secondary schools. The total hardware and software cost was $1.9 million dollars for an average of about $73,000 per laboratory. Initial training has been completed and there is now ongoing training of teachers as part of the regular computer program. A contract with the University of Montreal has been signed to evaluate the program. A recently signed loan agreement with the Central American Bank of Economic Integration will provide funding to install computer laboratories in all secondary schools and in 50 percent of primary schools. The loan is for $12.9 million, with US$3.4 million in counterpart funds for administration and training. Communities are being asked to pay for air conditioning.

In the Costa Rica program, a full-time teacher specially trained in informatics is responsible for each laboratory. On average, students from participating classes work in the laboratory twice a week. Computer classes are not mandatory and are provided only if the subject matter teacher is interested. In the Costa Rica program, Sketchpad is used in math, Superlink for multimedia presentations in social studies, Labpc for science, and Word and Paintbrush for Spanish. There is no specific computer curriculum, and computer activities are not included in the official subject matter curriculum. For this reason, ninth grade teachers are often reluctant to use the laboratory since it takes away time which could be spent preparing for national examinations. Nonetheless many students show a great deal of interest in computers. It has been reported that students often worked long after-school hours preparing reports such as multimedia descriptions of community and environment issues.

The computer laboratory in operation in the Liceo del Sur, a secondary school enrolling 1,000 students and located in a poor district of San Jose, is typical of the current program. The laboratory has 24 computers (IBM 486s) with a server. Software includes Word, Paintbrush, Excel, PowerPoint, Winlogos, Sketchpad, PCLab and Superlink. In a typical example, students were developing a dictionary of teenage Costa Rican words and phrases, using Word and Paintbrush. The teacher was hoping to combine the student-generated dictionaries into a single dictionary and then to compare it with similar dictionaries in other countries in Latin America. The students worked in pairs, were reasonably adept at manipulating Word, and lingered until the beginning of the next period to complete their work. Training was provided every Friday to interested teachers. The laboratory was also used in the afternoon by the technical stream of the upper secondary level and in evening by the Open University for technical courses. The school has a small but operational library (2,000 books, mainly old). Unfortunately, the science laboratory had been closed and had been replaced by a workshop for mentally handicapped students.

A very rough estimate of annual unit costs of the program is $38 per student. This assumes $22 per student in annualized capital costs ($73,000 for a school of 1,000 with a computer life of four years and a 10 percent discount rate), $6 for the costs of a full time technology teacher (estimated salary of $6,000), and $10 for training, maintenance and electricity (perhaps $10,000 per year). Overall this comes to 13 percent of the estimated annual cost of $300 per student in academic secondary schools in Costa Rica. These costs are significantly lower than those in Chile and Jamaica but are nonetheless significant.

Under a contract with the Government of Costa Rica, the University of Montreal is undertaking a comprehensive evaluation of the impact of the assessment on mathematics learning, science learning, logical thinking, expository writing, and attitudes towards schooling and technology. In addition, structured interviews will be undertaken with students, teachers, and school directors. The results will be incorporated into the expanded program currently underway.

SOME CONCLUSIONS

Costa Rica has the basic infrastructure needed for a computers in education program, including electricity in all schools as well as relatively well-trained teachers. In addition Costa Rica's computer program incorporates much of what is considered best practice in implementing an educational innovation—a strong and continuing national commitment, good central management, emphasis on training, slow start-up on a pilot basis, good feedback mechanisms, and focus on local participation and commitment.

One current and acknowledged problem is the lack of integration into the official subject matter curriculum. This question and related training and cost issues will eventually need to be addressed. While the encouragement of bottom-up experimentation is noteworthy, eventually standardization of approaches and contents will be needed. Finally, as in any innovation, as the program goes national some school directors, teachers, and communities may not be adequately committed to the program.

While costs are lower than similar programs in the region, it is still not clear whether computers are the most cost-effective means of increasing learning at the secondary school level, compared to providing additional library and laboratory facilities, training teachers, and so on. Nor is it clear that the provision of in-school computers and retraining existing teachers is the best way to provide computer literacy to students.

Costa Rica's program provides only minimum software and a maximum of two hours per week of computer labs for each student. On this basis, and given that the computer programs are not integrated into the curriculum, it is unlikely that the current assessment would find positive effects on cognitive skills. It would find at most a modest impact on improved critical thinking and creativity, on attitudes towards schooling, and on school retention. But there could well be changes in attitudes towards technology, attitudes toward schooling, and aspirations. In fact, if the program results in an increased number of students being directed to technical and mathematical careers rather than to humanities, law, and social science, then, given the expected higher economic returns to technical fields, the program could well pay for itself economically.

Data from the 1992 Household Survey provide an example of the potential economic payoff. The average salary of engineers at that time was about US$6800 per year, compared to $4500 for graduates in philosophy, arts, and letters, for a difference of $2300 per year. This means that the cost of providing computer instruction ($38 per student per year, or $114 over the three years of lower secondary school) could be recouped by society if no more than 1 percent of all secondary school students changed their profession from humanities to engineering (e.g., the gain to society would be $23 per year for the entire work life of a graduate).

In short, in spite of the above issues and uncertainties, the long term economic and social payoff of the Costa Rican program could well be significant. To verify this positive impact, future studies of cost-effectiveness of secondary school programs, should analyze changes in student learning and attitudes. In addition, they should assess the impact of computer programs on aspirations as well as (through tracer studies) on the actual occupations chosen by graduating students.

Section 3

The Success Stories: The Use of Distance Education in Out-of-School Education

The new global economy is demanding fundamental, rapid change in primary and secondary education, at the same time that the new technologies are offering dramatic new tools for learning. The way we work and the way we learn will change profoundly in the coming decades as a result.
(Clifford Block)

An epigram, coined at least a decade ago, is still relevant today: *Technology is the answer; what was the question?* It is easier to promote technology as the solution to educational problems if we define the problems vaguely, but this is not good enough for educational policy makers and governments.
(John Daniel/Anne Stevens)

Unlike previous major socioeconomic shifts, the current paradigm shift can be influenced by decisions which can shape, to a significant degree, the outcomes. (Linda Harasim)

"It is far better to show young children how to wash their hands than to tell them." In that statement is summed up much of the potential educational power of television, a power not limited to young children! (Clifford Block)

The knowledge media give us the opportunity to switch the spotlight from the classroom and teaching back to the individual and learning. (John Daniel/Anne Stevens)

Introduction

D istance education is the use of technology to partially or fully replace or augment the traditional classroom. In contrast to computers in education, distance education has been around for a long time, and has had demonstrable success in effecting educational change in a variety of contexts. The papers in this chapter summarize what is known about distance education, including the conditions for its success, and describe its wide applications.

Zimra Peled's experience using technology for education is encapsulated in a brief paper, **"Television in Education."** In 13 points, she summarizes the benefits and shortcomings of this medium as well as the activities for which it is a good vehicle.

"Mass Media in the Service of Latin American Education," by Clifford Block, provides a view of experience in distance primary and secondary education in three broad areas. In the first—improving the quality of education—there are examples of the use of television in South Carolina and El Salvador, the U.S.-based "Star" and 'Galaxy" programs, and interactive radio instruction in a number of developing countries, including eight in Latin America. In the second area—providing alternative access to basic and secondary education—Telesecundária in Mexico and Telecurso 2000 in Brazil successfully provide alternative secondary education opportunities through television. The third area involves reaching the general population, pre-school to adult, with informal education messages and relevant information for their lives. Examples include adaptations of "Sesame Street" for pre-school children and their caretakers. The keys to success for using mass media include designing an educational research and development framework; closely integrating media with activities of students, teachers, parents; and the use of learning materials.

"Success Stories: the Use of Technology in Out of School Education," by John Daniel with Anne Stevens, focuses on the use of technology for higher education. Daniel describes a "triple crisis" in higher education—rapid growth, high costs, and inadequate flexibility—that also represents an opportunity. Eleven "open" universities in the world now enroll more than 100,000 students each, including the UK Open University enrolling 150,000 and the Chinese Television University system enrolling more than 500,000. The unit costs of the eleven "mega-universities" are less than $350 per student, far lower than conventional university costs. The authors stress that distance higher education offers significant curricular diversity and flexibility. However, its success depends on high-quality multimedia learning materials, dedicated personal academic support for students, adequate logistic support, and a strong research and development base. In addition, distance education flourishes best when implemented by institutions separate from residential universities.

In **"Distance Learning and Technology in Brazil,"** João Batista Araujo e Oliveira reviews the history of distance learning in Brazil since the 1960s. It begins with television for formal and informal schooling and establishment of a non-profit educational television channel. This was followed in the 1970s and 1980s by national radio literacy programs, a national school equivalency program called Telecurso launched by Globo television, programs for rural areas and additional programs on a variety of subjects, and the early use of computers for training. In the 1990s, social marketing has increased, computers are increasingly used in schools, a national program for teacher training with interactive features has begun, and the City of Rio de Janeiro and the state of Minas Gerais have started television programs for students and for teacher training. In addition, the federal government recently financed the purchase of 50,000 television sets in primary schools and has begun a massive program to equip 6,000 schools with 100,000 computers. Overall in Brazil, effective and efficient uses of existing technology are prevalent outside of mainstream education, with applications for private use, open broadcasting, and training institutions.

"Telecurso 2000," by Joaquin Falção, summarizes the objectives and content of this innovative program begun in Brazil in early 1995. It is directed at adults who have not completed secondary education, preparing them for a secondary school equivalency examination. Subjects include those in a standard secondary curriculum (e.g., math, science, and Portuguese) as well as mechanics. The pedagogical approach emphasizes education for work, developing basic skills, citizenship, and contextualized teaching. Television, videocassettes, and print materials are used. Students have the choice of studying on their own, in classrooms, or with a mentor. In 1997, 110,000 students participated in 4000 Telecurso classrooms.

"The Internet and Intranets for Education and Training," by Linda Harasim, examines the potential for the Internet in education and training. The Internet promises to combine distance education and computers in education in a powerful new relationship. According to Harasim, in the 21st century the Internet will form the backbone of the knowledge economy.

Investment in these new structures is essential. There are promising applications and experiments in the USA, Canada, and Europe, including the Canadian Virtual U and Tele-learning Networks of Centers of Excellence. Education environments on the Internet and the World Wide Web should be customized to support knowledge work and collaborative learning.

In general the papers in this section show that the greatest successes of distance education have come in efforts to extend the school to underserved populations, as in the cases of the open universities and programs such as Telecurso. This success occurs because technology replaces in part or fully the traditional teacher and classroom, usually reducing costs, and the endeavor does not depend on an existing bureaucratic infrastructure. In contrast, successes inside formal primary and secondary education are fewer and more difficult, since technology by definition becomes an "add-on" cost and since the inertia of traditional classrooms, teachers, and regulations is difficult to overcome. However, the lowered costs of technology, combined with the experiences of some recent US programs and of interactive radio in developing country classrooms, suggest that successes may also be possible within the formal system.

Television in Education

Zimra Peled

Television can offer high quality educational programs. The following are the main features of this medium:

- Updated and information rich

- Visually and audio-visually manipulative

- Geared towards the needs of a wide ranging and heterogeneous clientele

- Consolidates and activates existing knowledge

- Replaces the teacher (when needed)

It is therefore an excellent vehicle for:

- Pre-school education
- Basic skills instruction
- Education for the disadvantaged
- Adult education (life-long education)
- Edutainment

However, it has short-
comings. In particular,
it does not offer an
interactive learning
environment. Therefore:

- It has a limited capacity to enhance
  the use of interactive communications.

- Mechanisms of collaboration are
  limited.

- Its capacity to enhance the develop
  ment of higher-order skills—the
  work tools of the "smart learner"—
  is limited.

Mass Media in the Service of Latin American Education

This is an extraordinary moment of possibility for education, with two powerful forces interacting. The new global economy is demanding fundamental, rapid change in primary and secondary education, at the same time that the new technologies are offering dramatic new tools for learning.

Clifford Block The way we work and the way we learn will change profoundly in the coming decades as a result.

IN AN ERA OF COMPUTERS AND THE INTERNET, WHY SHOULD EDUCATIONAL LEADERS CONTINUE TO BE INTERESTED IN THE BROADCAST MEDIA?

Given the momentum of the computer and networking revolution, educational innovators will be strongly tempted to move away from the technologies that seemed so revolutionary earlier, the mass media of radio and television. But in fact there are powerful reasons to embrace these media. First, they have been successful in many different contexts in stimulating rapid, systematic, and equitable educational change; secondly, in the process quite sophisticated methods

Dr. Block directs Block International Consulting Services, Berkeley, California.

for their use have been developed. With the addition of the newer technologies, and with a growing knowledge of learning processes, even more is attainable.

The demonstrable successes this paper reviews are wide-ranging. Millions of preschool children are involved each day with their friends at "Plaza Sesamo" or at other national versions of "Sesame Street." Hundreds of thousands are mastering the basics of math, language and other subjects more effectively through new, active-learning radio approaches. Millions of children are learning about science, math, language and the environment with the aid of satellite television broadcasts, some through completely new, child-centered approaches to learning. Adults are catching up on missed educational opportunities through televised instruction at their workplaces or homes. And the entire population of the hemisphere is informally learning skills ranging from better health and nutritional practices to what new information technologies are all about.

As leaders review this and other sources of information, they will be addressing the appropriateness of such strategies in relation to the fundamental tasks they face, namely:

- to quickly equip their populations for the skill-intensive and information-intensive economies of the next century;

- to provide fundamental educational skills for *all* their citizens, breaking through the barriers of poverty and isolation; and

- to provide for the continuing education that the economic future demands.

The evidence seems to show that use of the media holds substantial promise in terms of these objectives. It is not difficult to *plan* educational reforms, it *is* difficult to *implement* them. The wise use of media, together with the training and support needed to use them well, may help ensure effective implementation at reasonable costs.

What kinds of educational priorities have the media successfully addressed?

Applications to three areas of educational concern are reviewed throughout the paper:

1. Improving the quality of primary and secondary education.

2. Providing alternative access to basic and secondary education.

3. Reaching the general population, preschool to adult, with important informal education and information.

What have been the keys to success?

The key contribution of technology applies to the effective use of the media as well: The use of technologies in education can provide learning experiences that have been carefully developed, tested in many settings, and continually refined—which is simply not possible with most of the traditional components of education. There is a remarkable commonality in how most of the highly successful radio and television efforts have been designed.

1. They have used an educational research and development (R&D) framework in their creation, assessing success and failure through clear-eyed formative evaluation of the learning outcomes, and then making the adjustments needed for continuing improvement.

2. As fully as possible, they have closely integrated the media lessons with the activities of teachers, parents, peers and textbooks, providing teachers with the training they need to be effective.

3. They have overcome the potential passivity of watching and listening by stressing continual active participation in thinking and learning activities and by continually engaging their audience's attention, imagination, and curiosity, through educational formats as varied as music, stories, visual images, and humor.

4. They have stressed the relationship of learning with applications to the real world as experienced by the learner.

5. They have created a context where learners and teachers feel like participants and even partners, rather than merely the recipients of teaching.

Remarkably, these strategies have been applied successfully within widely different educational philosophies, from the highly structured "behaviorism" of the 1960s to today's child-centered, "constructivist" approaches. The examples to be discussed will illustrate that.

Their demonstrated success illustrates the greatest potential strength of all uses of technology: the capacity to incorporate the science of learning into day-to-day educational practice, under widely varying conditions. As that science unfolds, the educational media should be well placed to explore their practical utilization.

A note about the computer revolution

Computers and international networking have such enormous capabilities that it is certain they will exert a powerful effect on education.

But, in contrast to the media, we are just beginning to discover how to use them effectively. Many of the lessons discovered over the past decades about effective media use in educational reform will apply directly to strategies for developing these new tools as well.

These strategies will be noted in the following pages, as projects exemplifying them are reviewed.

WHAT SERIOUS EDUCATIONAL USES ARE BEING MADE OF RADIO AND TELEVISION BROADCASTING?

Key projects and what we have learned from them

This survey will begin with the use of educational media within school settings, then move on to "alternative" schools of those without conventional access. It will conclude with informal learning through the public media.

How have television and radio been used to improve primary and secondary schooling?—From comprehensive systems reform to child-centered inquiry

Over the past three decades, television's use has reflected change in educational thinking, from tightly structured approaches in the behaviorist model to recent "constructivist" strategies to stimulate student inquiry. There is evidence that well-designed implementations of both types have produced some substantial successes, and all have limitations.

Television as catalyst for the comprehensive, systems reform of educational sectors (Example: El Salvador)

In the late 1960s and early 1970s, TV was viewed as a way to rapidly produce dramatic, comprehensive educational change: to break through traditions of rote instruction, to introduce new curricula, to compensate for inadequately skilled teachers, and to do so rapidly. El Salvador's well-documented junior secondary school reform represented that approach. A complete educational redesign was carried out, with new curricula, daily television lessons in every core subject, text and classroom exercises linked to each daily lesson, and as much as a year of teacher retraining. The approach succeeded in many important respects. Evaluations showed successful introduction of the new curriculum, measurable gains in important student capabilities, and the use of new teaching methods such as learning science through experimentation. Furthermore, enrollment at the junior secondary level grew rapidly, a major national goal.

With a discontinuation due in part to political unrest, the ultimate longevity of this integrated strategy cannot be known. However, similar approaches were not sustained elsewhere (e.g., in the Ivory Coast, American Samoa, and Hagerstown, Maryland.) One persistent critique was the lack of autonomy provided for classroom teachers, and an over-reliance on the television teaching component. These systems also were somewhat limited instructionally. They did not build in continuing student activities and feedback, and made little use of formative evaluation. (In fact, those limitations were at the heart of efforts to design more adaptive systems such as interactive radio, to be described later.)

These highly integrated systems change efforts remain important, however. They show the unrivaled capability of technology to serve as a catalyst for very comprehensive change, and for achieving such change rapidly. In fact, the extent and rapidity of the reforms implemented by this strategy have few if any equals. The challenge today is to achieve this kind of integration while providing greater choice for teachers and more active involvement for students—a dilemma that has not been fully solved. Computer-based interventions face the identical dilemma.

Regional networking to equalize educational access across geographic, racial and economic boundaries (Example: South Carolina ETV)

Since the 1970s several states in the southern U.S. have carried out ambitious instructional broadcasting efforts, initiated to help equalize the quality of education available to rural children, who are predominantly poor and African-American. They permit greater flexibility in teacher utilization than those just described, and have persisted.

The South Carolina Educational Television Network, perhaps the leading system of this sort, broadcasts six thousand instructional television programs yearly—more than 200 each day. That enormous scope is made possible through the use of 32 dedicated satellite channels, as well as low-powered microwave transmitters which serve urban students. Both original productions and re-transmissions of numerous national programs are used.

As an integral part of the State's Department of Education, the programs are closely correlated with curricula, textbooks, and teacher guides. They seldom provide the entire core of instruction in a subject.

However, for topics such as the learning of Spanish by primary school children, they are a fundamental source of instruction.

The system is particularly valuable in introducing new curricula and reformed instructional methods. In recent months, for example, special teacher training series have dealt with the use of the Internet and with the implications of brain research for early childhood and infant education. These systems show how television can sustainably fill in continuing gaps for less advantaged schools by providing wide choice to individual schools, making use of everything nationally available, and designing targeted programs in new curricular areas, for both students and their teachers. These States have committed themselves to a comprehensive production and reception infrastructure, making the flexible educational use of the medium easy.

Strategies to serve varying local needs with national broadcast services (Example: Star Schools)

A different policy approach is represented by the U.S. "Star Schools" satellite-centered initiative. Star Schools began in 1988 as a Federal government program designed to employ the expanding coverage of satellites to help equalize rural educational opportunity, especially to provide courses in foreign languages and the sciences to rural schools that lacked specialized teachers. (Its sponsors argued that the U.S. was falling behind the innovative use of satellites for education in other countries, particularly in the developing world.). For a five-year start-up period, the Federal Government competitively funds groups to develop new distance education services. Future financing then depends on the purchasing of those services by state and local school systems.

The result has been the creation of a number of new educational networks, some regional and others national, which compete with each other or serve local and regional needs. These systems now serve 1.6 million students annually, in large urban areas as well as rural schools. The technologies have expanded to open broadcasting, audio- and video-conferencing, cable, fiber optics, videodiscs, fax, computers, and the Internet. Satellite television broadcasting, however, still predominates, although often with telephone feedback from participating classrooms.

Currently funded projects illustrate the evolving range of distance teaching uses that are supported. A university in Puerto Rico is developing teacher training and curricula for Puerto Rican students, focusing on computer literacy, technology, and the environment. A

California-based network is developing programs broadcast in Spanish to enhance parental involvement of recent immigrants. Several regional, state, and national networks provide courses in math, science, and technology, some tailored to specific needs such as students in inner cities. Finally, the Grand Canyon National Park is creating an environmental curriculum, integrated with math, the sciences, art, and the social sciences, all linked to the ecosystems of the Grand Canyon.

The Star Schools funding strategy has generated a multiplicity of distance education services, some tailored to regional needs and others to specific groups which are nationally dispersed such as rural or urban youth, or second-language speakers. Government funding is used to initiate new services, while the marketplace of school demand determines long-term viability.

New uses of television to bring "child-centered" education into the classroom (Example: The Galaxy Classroom)

The role of classroom television is gradually being redefined, to encompass new child-centered, "constructivist" approaches to teaching and learning. Many current broadcast courses are developing theme-based and inquiry-based approaches to the learning of science, language arts, and other subjects. The most ambitious of these new approaches is the "Galaxy Classroom" system.

Galaxy uses the new direct broadcast satellites to help bring child-centered curricula to primary school classrooms, particularly in the "inner cities" and rural areas of the U.S., where educational results are most discouraging. The project's focus has been on early science education, on language arts—improving the learning of reading, writing and the attendant mental skills of comprehension and communication—and on enhancing student confidence in their intellectual capacities.

Galaxy's technologies are an unusual combination of television, classroom facsimile machines, and videotape recorders, together with extensive teacher guides and student material for activities, reading, and science experimentation.

VCRs are used to record the television programs for repeated review. The facsimile network is key. It is used to encourage students to write in a realistic setting to learners at other sites and in response to queries posed by the characters in the televised Galaxy Classroom. Many educators consider the incentive to write critical to learning, particularly writing about personal interests. For this purpose, the fax is a more efficient than the use of multiple computers in each classroom, and one which does not require computer skills.

In Galaxy, television is not used for conventional instruction, yet it plays an absolutely key role. Its use is for introducing themes for language learning and for stimulating inquiry in science learning. All series are dramas, with a continuing cast of children engaged in exploration and scientific questioning (in the science series) or (in the language arts series) involved in discussions, arguments, and even fantasies as they explore issues affecting their young lives such as justice, personal privacy, and multi-cultural differences. The perspective is always that of young, poor, and often minority students. The TV programs are broadcast only at the beginning and end of several-week theme cycles, with the final program incorporating student comments. All other classroom time is then spent in activities related to the issues personified by the characters in the televised programs.

Galaxy was designed through major corporate investments in educational research and development by a nonprofit institute set up by Hughes Aircraft (a leading satellite provider), with additional Government (National Science Foundation) financing. A two-year, 38-site pilot effort perfected the system's educational and technical operation and produced a thorough impact evaluation.

The evaluations demonstrated significant gains in reading comprehension and vocabulary over control groups. In more difficult-to-assess analytic thinking skills, the evidence was also positive. Equally important, student and teacher enthusiasm for this new style of education was extraordinarily high.

Galaxy illustrates how the powerful storytelling capacity of television can be used to provide a context relevant to children for learning, self-expression, and inquiry. While the Galaxy curriculum provides structure and determines the pace of instruction, teachers select and guide the specific classroom activities, a satisfying role. The fax provides a unique mechanism for individual feedback and writing practice. Overall, Galaxy shows another way that the broadcast media can be used to stimulate active mental engagement—the fundamental step to effective learning.

The re-invention of instructional radio: Interactive Radio Instruction and the improvement of educational quality. (Examples: Several Latin American nations.)

Radio has long been used to transmit lectures to remote students. However, its development into a major strategic tool for improving the quality of learning has been more recent, the result of a sustained series of R&D efforts. Interactive radio was conceived in the 1970's by educational researchers at the U.S. Agency for International Development and Stanford University as a way to combine new knowledge about how students learn with the use of a low-cost delivery medium, radio. The result has been a series of primary school radio-delivered curricula characterized by continuous student learning activity during and after the daily broadcasts. Learners are continuously engaged in learning processes through questions, activities, stories, music, radio teachers and characters—all designed to engage their imaginations and to connect to their own experiences. Every activity builds on previous knowledge and periodically reviews it, using principles that research has shown to be important in mastering basic intellectual skills: distributed practice, constant feedback to learners, and learning within multiple contexts.

Today, several million learners are using Interactive Radio Instruction (IRI) each day in Latin America, Africa and Asia. IRI projects are currently underway in the Dominican Republic, Honduras, Bolivia, El Salvador and Venezuela, with pilot activities for various applications in Haiti, Ecuador, and Costa Rica. The IRI methodology has steadily been extended from original applications to primary school mathematics (in Nicaragua) to the learning of Spanish, English, health, Portuguese, science, ecology, early childhood education, and adult basic education.

No technological intervention has had more consistent evidence of its effectiveness. Evaluations have typically demonstrated very large learning gains over children in conventional classrooms, in every subject and in every region of the world. In several recent rural applications, the use of IRI has reversed the traditional urban-rural difference in achievement and has shown particular power in improving the scores of girls in math, science and language. Studies also have shown strong teacher enthusiasm for the approach, and great support by students.

Recently, IRI programs have extended to guiding the teacher as well as the student. For example, early childhood programs in Bolivia are training care givers as they interact with young children listening to the broadcasts.

The cost-effectiveness of IRI is exceptional. After initial development costs, annual implementation costs have typically ranged from $1.00 to $1.50 per student (with populations of several hundred thousand). A World Bank study found such cost-effectiveness to be appreciably greater than any other interventions with which it was compared, and a recent study by South Africa found IRI to be one-third to one-half the cost of other options for teaching English nationally. Since IRI broadcasts also generate large numbers of informal adult learners, its cost-effectiveness is actually even higher than formally measured.

Like other highly successful educational media efforts, IRI's development has been based on an educational R&D approach, making use of formative evaluation and revision. Its instructional strategies, such as engaging the learner through multiple formats, stimulating active learning, and providing constant feedback and review are applicable to all efforts to improve learning.

Interactive radio demonstrates two advantages of radio as opposed to other technologies. Radio's production costs are low enough to permit well-designed and tested local adaptations. Radio's dissemination costs are low enough to quickly reach large numbers of learners with improved teaching methods.

The utilization of public media in schools, and the growing complementarity of the mass media, computers, and the Internet

Linking general programming with school curricula. Several educationally relevant broadcast and cable television channels in the United States facilitate the use of their news, science and history programs within schools. "CNN in the Classroom," for example, provides discussion guides for teachers on relevant themes and prepares special composite programs for school audiences. Cable networks such as the History Channel and the Discovery Channel (which deals with science), also provide such assistance, including thematic analyses of their upcoming programs and suggested readings. In addition, there the many offerings of the Public Broadcasting Service and other networks whose primary functions are educational.

Governmental policies throughout the U.S. require local cable service providers to provide a free cable link to every school requesting one, a significant stimulus to the educational use of this growing reservoir of programming.

The growing interaction between the media and the Internet. Over the next decade, the mass media of television and radio will begin to merge with the interactive media of computers and the Internet. Interesting complementarities are already occurring. CNN, for example, provides schedules on the Internet for its upcoming "CNN in the Classroom" segments. For parents, the Internet provides daily synopses of each upcoming "Sesame Street" program, together with guides for parental activities, a Parents Forum, and video clips from the upcoming program. Perhaps most importantly, some television-based distance teaching networks are providing feedback opportunities for learners through Internet links.

The practicality of these hybrid and complementary approaches probably will evolve rapidly. For at-home learners, the interactive capability of the Internet will facilitate much more active involvement. For learners in school, television can provide structured, well-designed courses and rich visual experiences, while use of the Internet can encourage application of that knowledge to relevant inquiries and deepening of that knowledge.

How has broadcasting been used to extend educational opportunity through alternative learning contexts?

The very first serious uses of educational broadcasting were to provide education to those for whom traditional primary and secondary schools were not available. The famous Australian radio schools have for sixty years served those living in the remote Australian outback, and served them well. In the LAC Region, there have been several important initiatives using both radio and television.

The creation of radio schools for rural literacy (Example: The CIESPAL model, Colombia and other Latin American nations)

The use of radio to provide opportunities for achieving and sustaining literacy was developed originally in Colombia by the well-known CIESPAL project, and has been very influential. The approach combines radio lessons, family or community volunteers, and written materials, primarily in the form of specially designed rural newspapers. This basic approach has been replicated in most Latin American nations, in many cases through the sponsorship of the Catholic Church, which brings the added dimension of community outreach to the educational mix.

Millions have been well-served through these programs. As the systems have matured, they have gone beyond basic literacy to provide an array of information and basic skills important to individual economic development, health, and social development.

Keys to their enormous success have been the incorporation of several principles of effective learning:

- The literacy training is presented by providing information of genuine utility to the day-to-the day lives of rural people, particularly involving agriculture, health, and the family.

- The social support so essential to non-formal media education is provided by focusing on the family as the educational unit.

- The motivation to sustain and develop literacy skills is provided through specially produced "campesino" newspapers, full of useful information and written in a language designed to be comprehensible to new literates.

Providing alternative basic education to rural communities through interactive radio (Example: RADECO in the Dominican Republic)

Interactive radio has been adapted by the Dominican Republic to reach children in hill communities so remote that they have no access to conventional primary schools. The RADECO project (which now has been incorporated to serve larger segments of the Dominican population) provides the core of the first several grades of instruction through interactive radio broadcasts to students gathered in a community center (often a thatched hut) after the day's agricultural work is over. Tutors from the community assist the learners, who meet in multi-age groups for about 90 minutes each day. Evaluations have shown that students learning from interactive radio in these very basic conditions do at least as well as those in conventional classes in rural schools—and of course at a far lower cost.

Providing alternative secondary education through televison (Examples: Telesecundária, Mexico; Telecurso 2000, Brazil)

Telesecundária. One of the most successful and sustained distance education efforts in the world is Mexico's well-known Telesecundária program, initiated in 1968. Telesecundária is now an important component of Mexico's educational system, providing access to quality secondary education to 690,000 students throughout rural Mexico through a combination of television programming, books, and community-based teachers. It grows at a rate of almost 20 percent annually. Mexico's satellite capability has made possible ready access to students living in rural communities of less than 2,500, where access to conventional secondary education is particularly limited. Telesecundária today serves students in almost 12,000 schools.

In a landmark of international collaboration, Mexico's Ministry of Education, its domestic satellite authority, and several Central American nations agreed in 1996 to use Mexico's Solidaridad Satellite for international utilization of Telesecundária. Costa Rica is the first to implement such plans. Mexico is making available an invaluable store of 3600 fifteen-minute television programs and associated texts and teacher guides, which are being supplemented by Costa Rican programming.

Telesecundária is remarkable in its full institutionalization within Mexico's Ministry of Education, its continued commitment to both growth and quality, and the smooth coordination between community teaching resources and nationally produced educational programming. Its new regional outreach marks a breakthrough. By overcoming traditional resistance to the use of educational materials developed elsewhere and by combining those with local programming, the economies of scale inherent in educational broadcasting can be realized more fully.

Telecurso 2000. [See description on page 175.] Telecurso 2000 is an important new effort to address educational equity for adults. It recognizes the importance of social support for learners, through the tele-salas. (Without such support, dropout rates are historically extremely high in distance teaching.) By embedding learning in both practical terms and popular formats, the programs showcase some of the special advantages of television for such purposes. The collaboration of private industry and the media community may serve as an important model for many nations.

How have the media been harnessed for informal learning?

Using "edutainment" and social marketing in the service of public education

In every nation, children and adults spend many hours a week viewing television and listening to radio. There have been numerous efforts to use some of those hours for informal education through "edutainment." Networks such as Globo TV and others have frequently added dimensions to their entertainment programs that have had important social utility, dealing with such issues as family planning and urbanization. One of the most popular talk show hostesses in the U.S., Oprah Winfrey, recently added a discussion of current books to her daily program, which has a huge audience particularly among African- American women. Her success has been measured by the ascendence of quite serious books to the best seller list, serving entirely new audiences of readers.

Social marketing campaigns integrating the mass media with messages from health professionals are now widespread. They have shown that large-scale behavior change can be generated and sustained, and have been largely responsible for the widespread use of oral rehydration therapy and the dramatic growth of childhood immunization. A program using television, popular music recordings and teenage stars (Tatiana and Johnny) produced a remarkable response in the use of family planning services by teen-agers throughout Latin America—and a series of "top ten" records on the unlikely topic of responsible sexual behavior!

Reaching preschool children and their care givers with early education. (Example: Plaza Sesamo.)

Perhaps the best-known educators in the world today are "Plaza Sesamo's" friendly parrot, his "Sesame Street" equivalent, Big Bird, and their counterparts in 130 other nations, including 17 in Latin America. Everywhere they are enhancing the readiness of children for schooling and informing their relationships, attitudes, and personal development.

The secret to that wide-ranging popularity is the fully collaborative co-production of each adaptation, pioneered between the Children's Television Workshop and specialists from Mexico and other Latin American nations. The Latin American specialists have introduced different perspectives from those in the U.S. series, with greater stress on the family, on community cooperation, and on the expanded roles of women in society. Educationally, the Latin American leadership has emphasized problem-solving and reasoning to a greater degree. It also uses a different pedagogical approach than that of the U.S. version. A recent development has been the intertwining of health knowledge and behavior throughout the series, in collaboration with UNICEF. The next 130-program series, for which co-production has just been completed, will focus on ecology.

As with the other highly successful education media approaches discussed, CTW attributes its educational success to the use of a rigorous research and development model, with intensive preliminary research on its target population, the definition of specific educational goals, and extensive formative evaluation and revision.

A CTW researcher has noted that television's strength is its ability to model behavior, a dominant mode of learning for young children. "It is far better to show young children how to wash their hands than to tell them…" In that statement is summed up much of the potential educational power of television, a power not limited to young children!

SUGGESTED NATIONAL AND REGIONAL ACTIONS

A summary of the "state-of-the-art" in the use of the media for education

In summary, educators have developed effective methods for employing the media in:

- significantly improving the *quality of learning*, even for the most economically disadvantaged and geographically remote

- achieving *rapid and comprehensive reform* in curriculum, teaching methods, and learning outcomes

- providing *alternative modes of access* to primary and secondary education

- providing *access to subjects not otherwise available* in their communities

- engaging young children and their caregivers in *school readiness and early childhood education* through home viewing.

As these applications have been created, there have been fundamental discoveries about the effective use of the media:

- A research and development approach, focusing on learning outcomes, has been refined into a highly successful educational development strategy.

- The creative strengths of the media in engaging audiences have been successfully combined with the science of learning and teaching.

- The integration of media, curricular materials, and the role of the classroom teacher has been well-developed, both in highly structured and more inquiry-based educational strategies.

- Many ways to reduce costs have emerged, ranging from sharing program development costs to lower cost television delivery to the redevelopment of instructional radio.

What are some major opportunities and challenges for the future?

In view of these successful efforts, it is noteworthy that no nations except perhaps Mexico are yet using the media (or other technologies) as fundamental components of their educational systems. A basic constraint may be the perceived need to provide such educational services for all, just as teachers, schools, and common textbooks are provided for all. The scale of the undertaking can be daunting, and the re-allocation of scarce educational budgets is extraordinarily difficult.

Given those constraints, what can be done? While that is a task for national educational leaders, some thoughts follow.

Nationally

1. Most importantly, the planning of education reforms for the next century must routinely incorporate the use of both the media and computer technologies. We are at the stage when they should be considered co-equal with teacher training, school building, curricular reform, and textbooks, not as separate, short-term initiatives.

2. As national planners develop their "informatics" policies, it is critical that these encompass educational applications, and that the use of the media be included.

3. Consider very seriously the use of the media as the integrating factor in comprehensive reforms of curricula and teaching methods. The ability of the broadcast media to drive the integration of new teaching methods and materials has been well-demonstrated from the time of El Salvador's innovations to recent child-centered educational approaches such as Galaxy.

4. For high-priority educational problems, devise strategies that combine the advantages of the media with the advantages of computer-based instruction and networking. For example, the combination of interactive radio instruction in math and language with individualized computer-based learning might prove an exceptionally powerful

combination. Similarly, broadcast support may greatly accelerate the initial use of the Internet by those in school and at home.

5. Recognize the value of targeting different educational efforts to different populations. The growth of multiple media channels for both television and radio now permits that kind of differentiation.

6.Build on the capacity of radio and television to reach children and parents in their homes. There may be no other practical method, for example, for reaching parents with a message about their importance in stimulating the intellectual development of their children.

7. Ensure that new initiatives incorporate the educational research and developent methods that have proved so successful. In addition to the examples cited here, these approaches have been central to the great success of the British Open University and the Republic of Korea's superb educational system, created since the 1970s on the strong base of systematic R&D. As part of that process, continuing pilot experimentation should be ensured.

8. Work much more actively with industry in general and with the media and computer industries in using these technologies to create the new kinds of expertise that will be required in the future.

Regionally

1. Development agencies must re-examine their own sectoral and project planning procedures, to regularly encompass the integration of technology and media strategies.

2. Consider the establishment of a Technology and Media Forum, utilizing computer conferencing, the World Wide Web, and video-conferencing, in order to:

- learn from the emerging experience of others as to policies, experience in introducing innovations, and evaluation outcomes

- share mure fully the enormous body of relevant program material from the nations of the region

- work with international program providers, such as the news networks, to establish links to classroom activities, as is done in the U.S.

- explore the potential of joint program development, particularly in new areas of concern and with new teaching/learning techniques

- carefully and continually analyze the research base and the implications of new research (e.g., on brain function, early childhood development, accelerated learning methods, multiple intelligence approaches) for the use of technology and the media in education

- encourage far greater use of the public media for the support of educational change

Neither the broadcast media nor the newer computer technologies represent a panacea for educational problems. In no way will they replace the meeting of human minds that is the essence of much great teaching and learning. But they are remarkable new tools, and we are beginning to master their use. There is no longer any doubt that they are worthy of a fundamental commitment by educational leaders.

The Success Stories
The Use of Technology in 'Out-of-School' Education

With projects such as the secondary school radio project in Brazil, the Universidad Estatal a Distancia in Costa Rica and the Universidad Abierta in Venezuela, South

John Daniel with Anne Stevens

America established early successes in the application of technology to education at various levels, and exciting new initiatives are springing up all over Latin America.

In this paper we try to give the benefit of experience elsewhere in the world. We report success stories, examine how technology has been used to achieve success, and focus on out-of-school education—for which we use the term "distance learning." Most of the article talks about universities, where most of the key successes in the application of technology to out-of-school education have been achieved. But some of the lessons of those successes can be applied to education at other levels.

DEFINING SUCCESS

Reference to success stories implies that we have a clear idea of success. But success in what? What are the problems that we are trying to solve? We are reminded of an epigram—coined at least a decade ago—which is still relevant today: Technology is the answer; what was the question?

It is easier to promote technology as the solution to educational

Sir John Daniel is Vice Chancellor, and Mrs. Anne Stevens is Director, of the Center for Modern Languages, The Open University, U.K.

problems if we define the problems vaguely, but this is not good enough for educational policy makers and governments. If you are spending public funds to apply technology to education, you must start with a clear idea of what you want to achieve As another epigram puts it: If you do not know where you are going, any road will take you there. We begin, therefore, by defining some key problems. If technology can solve them it would deserve the accolade of success.

Higher education

In higher education there is a crisis—a triple crisis.

It starts with a crisis of access in the emerging markets (what we used to call the developing countries). If you take those countries together, they would require a large new campus university to open every week just to keep constant the participation rates in higher education. New universities are not being opened at this rate, so a crisis of access lies ahead. In the world as a whole half the population is under twenty years old. In some places the proportion of youngsters is much higher: nearly three-quarters of Palestinians and South Africans are under twenty. In Latin American countries,demand for higher education is growing rapidly. Without vigorous action many of these young people will grow up to be unemployed, unconnected and unstable. Mass training for employability is required and young people need help to acquire a framework of ethics and values.

In richer countries there is a crisis of cost. University education is becoming too costly for individuals and governments. Take the United States as an example. For an American family the cost of sending a child to college, adding up tuition, room and board, is approaching 15 percent of the median family income. That's up from 9 percent of median family income 15 years ago. The cost of sending your offspring to a public university is 15 percent of income. If you pick a private university the figure is nearly 40 percent of median family income, up from just over 20 percent in the same fifteen year period. Americans are having difficulty coping with these costs. The crisis of access in poorer countries will not be solved with this expensive model.

The third crisis, visible the world over, is a crisis of flexibility. Rapidly changing labor markets are making universities ask themselves if they are teaching the right programs; they are reviewing the appropriateness of their curriculum. A steadily changing student body, including more adult learners in employment, is making universities question how they teach. For many students, classroom lectures on a fixed timetable are not the preferred mode of learning.

These crises are deeply worrying. But let us remember that the ideogram for *crisis* combines the signs for *danger* and *opportunity*. There are dangers, but let us also look for the opportunities. Technology is one.

Schools

So much for some general problems facing universities. What about the schools? One of us (JD) is vice-president of the International Baccalaureate Organisation. The IBO operates a diploma program for the senior years of high school in 70 countries, has just added a middle-years program and will soon offer a program for the primary years. Technology could help the International Baccalaureate (IB) face a number of challenges.

First, there is the challenge of operating efficiently a world-wide curriculum development and examination system. The continued credibility of an expanding International Baccalaureate relies on cost-effective administration. Technology has obvious applications. Second, the quality of the International Baccalaureate depends on the continuing professional development of those who teach it. The global distribution of IB teachers is a special challenge in this context. Third, the International Baccalaureate must have up-to-date curriculum resources, especially for subjects like the *Theory of Knowledge* which are unique to the program. Fourth, getting young people to work together across frontiers is a goal of the International Baccalaureate that is shared by many other schools. Can technology help there? Finally, what about distance education? Should the International Baccalaureate and other school-level programs be taught at a distance and, if so, for what purpose?

We are skeptical about using distance education for ordinary primary and secondary schoolchildren. Of course, organizations such as France's Centre National d'Enseignement à Distance (CNED), the Open School in India and the Correspondence School in New Zealand address these age groups successfully. However, they do so primarily for children in special circumstances. CNED was set up to help the children evacuated from the French cities in World War II and now enrolls those who cannot, for reasons such as illness or overseas postings, attend regular school. The Correspondence School in New

Zealand performed a signal service when epidemics shut down the regular schools. These are important success stories in the use of technology for out-of-school education.

However, they are also exceptions which prove the rule that the process of socialization, that is such an important function of primary and secondary schools, should involve frequent contact with adults and other children where possible. The technology of distance learning can help with the training of teachers and the provision of curriculum materials but we do not believe it should replace conventional schools for those children who are able to attend them.

IDENTIFYING SUCCESS STORIES

The preceding section has identified some criteria for success in the application of technology to out-of-school education. The central challenge is to widen access to education and training by reducing costs or increasing flexibility—preferably both. The development of flexible and inexpensive ways of providing pre-service and in-service training to teachers would have a large beneficial impact on schools, as would the development of curricular materials that could enable individual teachers to teach a wider range of subjects effectively.

Against these criteria the most sparkling success story in the use of technology in out-of-school education is the mega-universities.

The Mega-Universities

The mega-universities, which we define as distance teaching universities enrolling over 100,000 students, are perhaps the most important educational phenomenon of our time (Daniel, 1996). That is because the mega-universities address all of the crises in higher education listed above. Here, to support this claim, is a table listing the eleven mega-universities and giving some basic data about them. (Table 1)

First, in the countries that have created them, the mega-universities have greatly expanded access to higher education. Take two examples, the U.K. and China. There are 150,000 students in the U.K. Open University this year. In 1963, the year that the creation of the Open University was first proposed, there were only 130,000 students in all British universities combined. In China, where more than half a million people now study at degree level in the Television University

Table 1. The mega-universities.

COUNTRY	NAME OF INSTITUTION	EST.	ABBR.
China	China TV University System	1979	CTVU
France	Centre National d'Enseignement à Distance	1939	CNED
India	Indira Gandhi National Open University	1985	IGNOU
Indonesia	Universitas Terbuka	1984	UT
Iran	Payame Noor University	1987	PNU
Korea	Korea National Open University	1982(1)	KNOU
South Africa	University of South Africa	1873(2)	UNISA
Spain	Universidad Nacional de Educación a Distancia	1972	UNED
Thailand	Sukhothai Thammathirat Open University	1978	STOU
Turkey	Anadolu University	1982	AU
United Kingdom	The Open University	1969	UKOU

Notes:
1. As the Korea Air and Correspondence University
2. As the University of the Cape of Good Hope

System, the 1.5 million people who have graduated from its programs in the last decade represent 17 percent of the national output of 3-year degrees.

Second, some comparative figures illustrate the cost advantage of the mega-universities (Daniel, 1996:32). The 3,500 colleges and universities in the U.S.A. have an enrolment of 14 million students and annual spending on higher education is around $175 billion. That represents an average cost of $12,500 per student. The U.K. has 182 higher education institutions, 1.6 million students, and a spend of nearly £10 billion. It works out at around £6,300 per student, or about $10,000 which is comparable to the figure for the U.S.A. The eleven mega-universities enroll, between them, some 2.8 million students. Their budgets aggregate to a bit less than $1 billion. That works out at less than $350 per student. There is, therefore more than an order of magnitude difference between mega-university costs and either the U.S. or U.K. costs. In India, for example, we calculate that the per student cost at IGNOU is less than $100 per year. That is highly competitive in world terms.

Third, to those considerable advantages in access and cost, the mega-universities also add the advantage of flexibility. Distance education is an inherently flexible form of teaching and learning which puts fewer constraints of time and place upon students than classroom attendance. The evidence now shows that the quality of teaching and learning at a distance can be at least as high as on campus. For example, in Britain's national system for the assessment of teaching quality in universities the Open University has received an 'excellent' rating for most of its programs. At the moment it ranks number 10, out of 77 English universities, for the quality of its teaching—just behind University College London, which is in ninth place.

We also stress that distance education in general, and the mega-universities in particular, offer curricular flexibility. If a program is needed in a new area, the mega-universities make it possible to offer it to large numbers of people, all over the country, relatively quickly and to a high level of quality. A few years ago, for example, the U.K. government wanted a program that would make it possible for people in mid-career, particularly those with a science or technology background, to train as primary and secondary teachers. The Open University put on such a course. It is now the largest teacher-training program in the U.K. and in 1997 won the Queen's Anniversary Prize for higher education in recognition of its success. This was the first time that Britain's highest award of excellence for universities has been given to a teacher training program.

In the area of curricular flexibility, the most revolutionary academic advance of the last twenty years was made in Hong Kong. This was the creation, in the 1980s, of the Open College of Hong Kong. It began as a private institution based on the novel idea that with distance education you can import courses instead of exporting students. Although over forty open universities have been created around the world since the U.K. Open University was established in 1969, most have followed the Open University's example in developing their own distance courses from scratch.

The revolutionary idea in Hong Kong, pioneered by the late Don Swift, was to decide that since these other universities had developed a large range of courses across all disciplines, Hong Kong did not need to do so. It could simply buy the best courses and concentrate on supplying the infrastructure and student support that is essential for success in distance education. The Open College built up a degree curriculum based on courses imported from New Zealand, Australia,

Canada and the U.K.. At first the authorities were a bit suspicious, but people in Hong Kong are pragmatic and intelligent. In the late 1980s the government took over the concept itself and created the Open Learning Institute, which the Legislature renamed the Open University of Hong Kong in May 1997.

By this means, Hong Kong has given itself an additional university of 20,000 students for a tiny fraction of the cost of the other universities in the Territory. Indeed, since the operating costs will be paid entirely by student fees, the only charge the Open University of Hong Kong makes on public funds is the occasional capital investment. Most importantly, low cost is combined with high quality. For example, the MBA program of the Open University of Hong Kong is not only the largest MBA program in the Territory but also, in the judgement of many, the best.

A similar example of the use of course materials in other environments comes from the Modern Language program of the U.K. Open University. This is now the largest university language program in Britain and required the training of a large number of tutors all over the country. Once materials had been developed for tutor training they proved valuable for instructors teaching languages in conventional universities, where there has been a rapid growth in demand for language learning in recent years.

LESSONS FROM SUCCESS STORIES

The mega-universities clearly satisfy the key criteria for assessing success stories in the application of technology. The key to their success is distance education. However, since discussions of distance education are often clouded with confusion, we should explain it. Confusion arises because there are two different concepts of distance education. Furthermore those with one concept are often unaware that the other concept of distance education exists. This means that international discussions of distance education can be dialogues of the deaf. Latin America is particularly vulnerable to confusion because the United States has one concept of distance education while Spain and Portugal have the other. What are these two concepts?

The U.S. Congress Office for Technology Assessment defines distance learning as: "linking of a teacher and students in several geographic locations via technology that allows for interaction." That is a fair summary of what most Americans think distance education is, namely simultaneous audio- or video-conferencing to a set of remote classrooms. But that is not how the rest of the world conceives distance education.

Here's a definition from South Africa. It's longer, but also richer: "Distance education is the offering of educational programmes designed to facilitate a learning strategy which does not depend on day-to-day contact teaching but makes best use of the potential of students to study on their own. It provides interactive study material and decentralised learning facilities where students can seek academic and other forms of educational assistance when they need it."

What are the differences between these two concepts of distance education? They can be summarised in three points.

1. There are only two approaches to distance education: one targets individual learning; the other focuses on group teaching. Whatever terms people invent, distributed learning, correspondence study, flexible learning, home-study, remote-classroom teaching, tele-education, guided study, or whatever, distance education still boils down to these two traditions—and they are very different.

2. The most important difference is that the group teaching approach is based on synchronous communication. Teachers and students must communicate in real time. The individual learning approach is based on asynchronous communication. You create the university in the student's home so they can study there when it suits them.

3. Another important consequence follows. In the group teaching scenario the teacher communicates with students in a network of classrooms in real time. It is a teacher-centered form of education. That's not pejorative. It's simply a fact that if you try to set up a system for a teacher to address a number of remote groups you must design it from the teacher's point of view. Under the individual learning scenario you re-create the campus in thousands of homes—so it has to be a student-centered approach. You must design an effective home learning environment for the student.

Those three points are all you need to know in order to use distance education strategically. Each tradition of distance education has its own strengths and weaknesses. We believe that the individual learning approach offers a more powerful response to the crises of access, cost and flexibility. That is because it lends itself, more than the group teaching approach, to wider access, lower cost and greater flexibility.

Evidence to support this assertion comes from the mega-universities. All of them, except one, focus on the individual at home or at work. That is the basis of their impressive achievement of offering flexible higher education to tens of thousands of students at low cost. But what about the exception, which is the China TV University? This is the world's largest learning system. Unlike the other mega-universities, where the students study mostly at home, the CTVU is a satellite-to-classroom operation. It also differs from the other mega-universities in having a very large full-time staff—including 18,000 full-time faculty where most of the other mega-universities have less than a thousand.

Some policy makers in China are concerned that the China TVU is gradually breaking up into a multi-campus network of face-to-face teaching universities, which will dull its cutting edge of low cost and consistent quality. The problem seems to be that students want more support than the televised lectures provide and there is a tendency to hire extra local staff to provide extra lectures. In the asynchronous form of student-centered form of distance education student support is built into the system, which makes it easier to expand the system cost-effectively.

On the present evidence of distance education in the mega-universities it appears that using asynchronous media to facilitate individual student learning has generated more success stories than using synchronous communication to teach groups. If that is true, how do we maximize the success of the asynchronous approach with students? A consensus is emerging about the four vital ingredients that are necessary.

First, students must have high quality multi-media learning materials. Study materials must be excellent and varied to make the campus in the home or the workplace a congenial university experience. Experience shows that using multi-skilled academic teams to produce such materials gives the best results. That, of course, is more expensive, which is why it is helpful to conduct distance education on a large scale.

Second, students perform best if they get dedicated personal academic support. For example each U.K. Open University student has their own tutor for each course, one of OU's 7000 adjunct faculty. They comment on and mark the student's assignments, hold group meetings and give support by phone and e-mail.

Third, efficient logistics are vital. Each individual student must receive the right materials and information at the right time. With over 100,000 students, that requires careful attention to detail.

Fourth, a strong research base is essential. When thousands of students use the materials for each course and millions of people view each TV program the content must be academically up to date. Here again, institutions with big economies of scale have the resources to move the academic paradigms steadily forward and create learning environments that are more intellectually exciting.

LOOKING AHEAD

But do we need to choose between these two approaches to distance education? Are not new technologies bringing these two approaches together? Let us examine the potential of a new generation of technology to make out-of-school education successful. First, what do we mean by new technology?

The Knowledge Media

Following our colleague Professor Marc Eisenstadt, we shall call these new technologies the *knowledge media*. He coined the term to denote the convergence of computing, telecommunications and the cognitive sciences. He did so because he claims that the *knowledge media* change the relationship between people and knowledge in a fundamental way.

Others have invented different terms: telematics; the information superhighway; multi-media and so on for these new combinations of information and communication technologies. Eisenstadt's term challenges us because he believes that the combination of present technologies with what we know about learning will change fundamentally the relationship between people and knowledge. That's because the knowledge media are about the capturing, storing, imparting, sharing, accessing, creating, combining and synthesising of knowledge. The knowledge media are not just a technical format, such as CD-ROM or computer conferencing, but the whole presentational style, the user interface, the accessibility, the interactivity. The knowledge media fit nicely with the modern view that science is less a statement of truth than a running argument.

All universities are now asking themselves what the knowledge media mean for them. Academics are effervescing with individual projects. In the western United States the governors dream of merging higher education into a great collective virtual university. But will it ever be real? To make it real we need to understand that the knowledge media give us the opportunity to switch the spotlight from the classroom and teaching back to the individual and learning. Universities are discovering that with good learning materials, effective networks and proper support, students can learn better at home than in class.

In looking at the potential of the knowledge media to fuse together the two traditions of distance education into a framework for university education in the new millennium, we need to remember our earlier list of the four qualities that make distance education successful for individual students: stimulating materials; individual support; good logistics and a research culture.

How can the knowledge media reinforce these elements of quality and impact? It's too early for definitive statements because in a distance education system—indeed in any mass university system—you can't really get the benefits of technology until most students own the necessary equipment. Ownership of modem-equipped computers is increasing fast in the richer countries, but even there it cannot be taken for granted.

The other sensitive issue is whether electronic communication through text, even if it is backed up by video pictures of those communicating, can really be as effective as the current tutorial systems. The main function of U.K. Open University tutors has always been to mark and write comments on students' assignments. This can be made much faster—and more iterative—by electronic mail. However, the feeling that your tutor lives in your region and may, if numbers warrant, hold face-to-face tutorials is psychologically important. So the U.K. Open University is proceeding cautiously, particularly as far as overseas activity is concerned.

Even so, the U.K. Open University is beginning to use the knowledge media at industrial strength. This year it has 30,000 students networked from home. Although only one-fifth of the student body, those are still large numbers of students. One course alone has 3,500 students communicating over the network.

The key feature of networking is that it displays a desirable characteristic of distance education: big is beautiful. The Law of the Telecosm, otherwise known as Metcalfe's Law, states that the value of a network to its users rises as the square of the number of users. At the U.K. Open University we see that law in action. We have a class of 1,000 each year in our teacher training program. They are all networked and it is true that the interactions between this rich tapestry of humanity are ten thousand times richer than if there were only 10 in the class.

The Law of the Telecosm creates a real breakthrough in distance learning. Hitherto, with so-called interactive media such as video-conferencing, the interactive value went down sharply as student numbers went up. Suddenly we have an interactive medium where that is not true. More students means richer communication and support. In the earlier phase of distance education, based on the mass media, more also meant better, because economies of scale allowed bigger investments in learning materials. The problem, explored nearly twenty years ago by Daniel and Marquis (1979), was that economies of scale broke down for the vital interactive activities. With computer networking that restriction disappearing.

That is why the U.K. Open University is investing so much effort in scaling up these interactive Internet technologies. It is able to enrich and extend distance learning by creating a web of student-to-student communication and by giving guided access to academic resources that students could not otherwise use. What is being done, in effect, is to add the essence of video conferencing to the tool kit of the individual learner. But the main drawback of video-conferencing, which is the need to assemble students in groups—and therefore the impossibility of scaling it up—has been eliminated. However, we do not claim that this is the total answer to distance learning.

In the last twenty-five years over two million people have studied with the U.K. Open University. The main lesson it has learned from all those students, a rich tapestry of humanity, is that there is no magic single medium. People are different and the mix of media they like to learn from is different. What the Internet and the World-wide Web do, helped by some of the technologies being developed at the Open University such as the Knowledge Media Institute Stadium, is to provide a communicative glue that increases the synergy between the other media.

Distance education has already produced the most promising academic development of our times, the mega-university. Thanks to the emergence of the knowledge media the third millennium will see distance learning take the central role in university life that classroom teaching has occupied in the second millennium.

Distance Learning and Technology in Brazil

Distance learning has a long tradition in Brazil, beginning over 60 years ago with the innovative programming of radio pioneer Roquette Pinto. Non-formal educational programs, mostly geared to

João Batista Araujo e Oliveira

adults, were broadcast by the public radio station he helped create.

THE SIXTIES

Private correspondence schools flourished in the 1950s and 1960s. The courses were based primarily on printed materials, plus some special kits for technical courses in such areas as electricity and mechanics, where special training materials are required. Tutors graded the exams and papers and sent feedback to students through the mail. Several million students registered for such courses, which implied a real demand and a genuine benefit to their clients.

In the 1960s, radio was widely used for adult literacy programs. This was the decade of adult literacy, and the Catholic Church was intensely involved in mass education. MEB—Movimento de Ação de Base—sponsored several such initiatives throughout the country, occasionally with the help of the government. After the military coup in 1964, radio was used as a part of a movement to increase social awareness.

The advent of television in the late 1960s prompted large-scale television use for educational purposes within schools.

The state of Maranhão, in Northeastern Brazil, pioneered these

---

The author is president of the consulting firm JM Associados and Director of Instituto Brasil Seculo XXI.

efforts. TV programs served as the basis for expanding compulsory schooling from 4 to 8 years. Since qualified teachers were not available, classes were taught via TV and tutors worked with students using instructional materials prepared specifically for the TV courses. This program reached several thousand students each year, and is still active. The same idea was later introduced in the neighboring north-eastern state of Ceará.

At the same time, a private television channel owned by the Manchete Group, led by Gilson Amado, began broadcasting literacy and formal equivalency programs for adults. These initiatives became the basis for creating a national educational television channel in Rio de Janeiro in the late sixties, as well as a central body to coordinate tele-education, PRONTEL, in 1971.

The other significant event of this decade was the creation of TV-Cultura in São Paulo, which still operates primarily as a general educational TV channel. It has consistently produced excellent programming for children, as well as a small number of instructional programs.

THE SEVENTIES

During the 1970s, some of these traditions were reinforced and some were also centralized—just as everything else was being centralized in Brazil.

The major national project was Projeto Minerva, geared toward students graduating from the other national literacy program, MOBRAL. Minerva was based on a national radio network—all radio stations were required to broadcast this program at the same time. It offered equivalency programs for both primary and secondary education. PRONTEL, the national coordinating agency, also sponsored various initiatives from the recently created educational television stations in several states.

In the early 1970s, the National Space Agency (INPE—Instituto Nacional de Pesquisas Espaciais) pushed the federal authorities to sponsor an ambitious satellite-based in-school instructional program, Projeto SACI. This program was conceived as part of the ASCEND report developed in Stanford, California in 1967, and called for the intensive use of satellites to solve social problems. A pilot project was started in Northeastern Brazil and satellite connections were even tested over the course of the year, but the program never got off the ground, for a number of political and technical reasons.

The seventies were also the decade of instructional design and individualized instruction. Training institutions like SENAC started a number of instructional programs. The most impressive development was the transformation of an entire training school (SENAI/Rio) into an institution which offered individualized, self-paced instructional programs to thousands of students.

Large-scale private initiatives were also underway. The Landell de Moura Foundation continued its educational radio programs to cater to both rural and urban populations. The private network Globo launched a major equivalency program, Telecurso, which is still operating in the mid-nineties, and which reaches millions of people (in an open broadcast format), including thousands of formally enrolled students.

While GLOBO produces and broadcasts these programs (on their own channels and through educational television networks), public and private operators organize orientation sessions for new students. The most important program associated with Globo's Telecurso is sponsored by Fundação Bradesco, which offers such Telecourses to over 12,000 students per year, and which has shown extremely successful results.

GLOBO also sponsored the production and adaptation of "Sesame Street," in partial collaboration with TV-Cultura of São Paulo. On the basis of the success of this program, GLOBO produced a series based on the stories of popular children's writer Monteiro Lobato, "Sitio do Pica-Pau Amarelo," which was exceeding popular during the 1970s and early 1980s.

Another major private sector initiative was Projeto Logos II, a distance learning program for training teachers. This continues to be one of the most successful programs ever implemented in Brazil for in-service teacher training. The project includes printed materials for individualized, self-paced instruction, learning centers for student support, and sophisticated evaluation and administrative mechanisms. Projeto Logos II was developed by CETEB—a private educational institution — and its actual implementation was sponsored partially by local governments. Logos II was also modified to train off-shore oil technicians from PETROBRÁS on a cost-effective basis.

THE EIGHTIES

In the 1980s, technology was put to new uses, in addition to those conventional programs described above.

As the central role of the federal government diminished, some initiatives started at the state level, among federal universities and private providers. The major federal initiative was a special program in the area of computer software production. Funds were made available for projects which built up centers and produced programs. This program never really managed to get off the ground and, therefore, made no significant impact.

The use of open broadcasting for non-formal education became very important. Globo Rural and later entries such as Globo Ciência, Pequenas Empresas Grandes Negócios and similar programs, played and continue to play an important role in the dissemination of information and technology, in areas such as agriculture, business, management and production techniques. Audiences for these programs are counted in the millions. Globo Rural also introduced interactive TV, in which hundreds of viewers would write to the producers, to the agencies, or to specific projects shown on the program for further information and/or technical assistance.

Video tapes became a standard feature in training packages and training programs, and dozens of production centers, mostly private, were set up to provide such services.

Slowly, computers found their way into education, but mostly as motivational devices used in training programs. Simulations also started to be used as part of business training programs. Small-scale experiments flourished in schools (mostly private), training organizations and private firms.

Brazil's policy of tariff barriers had the double effect of raising hardware prices while building up local capacities in the areas of hardware, software development and equipment maintenance. The stiff tariffs may also have served as an additional incentive for hackers to begin pirating software and passing along other knowledge which was quickly disseminated throughout the country.

As more powerful technologies developed, business and governmental agencies started using satellites for tele-conferences. Even though no systematic use was made of this technology, the infrastructure and the technology were put into place, and teleconferencing has now became a routine practice in many organizations. EMBRATEL, the state owned telecommunications agency, has set up over 50 teleconferencing centers in Brazil for these purposes.

THE NINETIES

Three major developments of the 1990s are worth noting: the use of social marketing techniques for educational and social change, the dramatic increase in computer use, and some improvements to the practice of distance learning programs.

Social marketing is used both in programs which target a specific audience (on breast feeding, for example), and as a vehicle to shape new behaviors and attitudes. Popular soap operas are the preferred instrument to disseminate new values, such as attitudes toward sex or gender issues (including AIDS). They are also employed as a means to form positive attitudes toward schooling and basic education. The campaign Só a Escola Corrige o Brasil, sponsored by the private Foundation Odebrecht, for example, was a major media campaign launched around the time of the local and presidential elections to introduce the importance of basic education. The idea behind such efforts is not to promote alternatives to basic education, but rather to use media to improve the demand for better quality education.

Computers continue to be introduced in both public and private schools. The use of more sophisticated technologies, including CD-ROMs and the Internet, has become a reality in educational and training institutions of greater means. Commercial, educational and government initiatives are also booming throughout the country. The Federal University of Rio de Janeiro, among many others, has created laboratories to experiment with and encourage computer use at all educational levels. One private school in São Paulo, Bandeirantes, created a software house to produce, adapt and distribute educational software. The University of São Paulo has launched an innovative program called Escola do Futuro, which combines research, training and dissemination of innovative and successful practices for introducing computers in schools. Fundação Roberto Marinho, an arm of TV-Globo, has developed a special program to introduce the use of video technology in schools—Video-Escola—which presently reaches thousands of schools and teachers throughout the country.

Improvements have also been made in distance education. The federal government launched a national program for teacher training with several interactive features, Salto para o Futuro, which reached a wide audience and was very popular. In 1995, the federal government also launched a new TV channel for schools using satellite transmission facilities. The government financed the acquisition of TV-sets, reception antennas and video-tape recorders to virtually all urban public schools in the country, covering over 80 percent of the student population.

At the local level, there are examples of both successful and less successful initiatives. Multirio, created for the City of Rio de Janeiro, developed an interesting program for both teachers and students in the municipal school system. The state of Minas Gerais is presently launching a massive training program for the state's 140,000 teachers, using a combination of individualized instruction, mass media, and distance learning with local support. Pitágoras-TEC is also launching an innovative teacher training program for primary schools, using satellite broadcasts, in-school organized groups, Internet-based support, and private-sector sponsorship.

As the century draws to a close, Brazil still has many challenges to overcome. The incorporation of information technology in formal education programs is one. The role of information technology in education is minor, indeed, and has been demonstrated successfully only in training and non-formal education programs.

IN CONCLUSION

Visitors to Brazil would be impressed by the dual reality they observe in the overall economy, in education, and in the field of information technology in particular. The most modern infrastructure for and uses of high technology coexist with one of the world's most inequitable (and poor) educational systems. A recent survey of undergraduates revealed that 50 percent of their households have a micro-computer. Internet subscribers are counted in the millions, and cable television use is expanding at an incredible rate.

The results are very clear. Effective and efficient uses of existing technology are prevalent outside of mainstream education. In sectors that are either unregulated, or less regulated by government, new technologies have made their way. This is the case with private use, open broadcasting, training institutions of various kinds, and even in the area of non-formal education. Whenever a sector is regulated, as is the case with formal education, the resulting technologies are minimal or insignificant.

All kinds of barriers still exist which inhibit the introduction of new information technologies to education. Tariffs and governmental protection make telecommunication imports and services far more expensive than in other countries. Education is not financed in a way which induces efficiency, thus leaving few incentives for efficient uses of technology. Cultural barriers also exist—such as prejudices against distance education held by teachers who lack familiarity with new technology.

Even in the case of distance education, for which the country has strong capabilities and a long tradition, government regulation still prevents its widespread use. The federal government has been blocking the development of distance education to placate the prejudices and corporate interests of established institutions. New regulation being proposed is still inadequate for making distance learning as widespread as it is in other countries.

Most importantly, there is a general lack of incentives for schools to introduce technologies which would increase their efficiency. Until such incentives exist, pilot programs alone will demonstrate the potential impact of technology, and serve a useful learning function. The actual impact of this technology will have to wait until educational institutions have the incentive to become more effective and efficient.

Telecurso 2000
Breaking with the Paradigm of Traditional Education

Joaquin Falcão

It is a well-known fact that the field of education has been resistant to technological innovation. In Brazil, many authors have discussed this issue. It has not been easy to change educational practices and attitudes within this field. External pressures arising from a workplace where technology has advanced at a rapid pace make it imperative that educators change the way they do things. The adult education program known as *Telecurso 2000* is a part of that process, and the evidence shows that it is playing a major role in the effort to break with outdated concepts and traditional approaches to education.

In the classroom, students are systematically encouraged to be a subject of the learning process. Subject matter is explored through plausible situations taken from real life, in order to make it meaningful to the students and contextualize course content as regards the cognitive-affective relationship and the historical-critical approach to education. Learning is often permeated with value judgments, so as to encourage students to see themselves as citizens (illustrating the potential of emancipation education). Electronic resources (television, videotapes) are used not as complementary tools but rather as an integral part of

Joaquin Falcão is Executive Secretary of the Roberto Marinho Foundation.

the teaching process, reinforcing the alliance between education, technology and mass education.

Thus, Telecurso 2000 serves not only as a tool of distance education for students from the underprivileged classes but also as a means to upgrade learning in the regular educational system. At the very least, this approach to curricular development has shown how outdated expositional teaching methods are.

Telecurso 2000 has had such a positive impact on the Brazilian population, with thousands of congratulatory letters and telephone calls, that three new curriculum enrichment disciplines will soon be made available — environmental education, physical education and art.

This paper describes the educational context in which Telecurso 2000 was developed and the different stages in the production process and the dissemination of the course throughout the country. This program is particularly important because it has begun to be accepted as a legitimate distance education option that can help reduce the number of people who lack a basic education.

BACKGROUND

The main topic discussed at the forty-fifth Conference on Education sponsored by the United Nations Educational, Scientific and Cultural Organization was "The role of educators in a changing world." The basic working paper presented to participants included a listing of problems, prospects and priorities to be considered in strengthening the role of educators. Among others, the working paper mentioned the following challenges that must be addressed by any educational system wishing to achieve the goal of preparing people for life: the technological revolution, participation in democracy, and population growth.

In the case of Brazil, these challenges have been quite evident. With a population of nearly 155 million (three times the population of a few decades ago), this country recently (during the 1980s) emerged from a military regime and society began to take part in determining its own destiny. It still has pockets of poverty, especially in the north and northeast, as well as highly developed areas, mainly in the south and southeast. More than anything else, it needs to find creative ways to expand and consolidate its development.

The search for solutions is not an easy task, inasmuch as the country has a legacy of long-standing problems, including illiteracy (16 million inhabitants -IBGE/1995) and incomplete schooling (20 million inhabitants -*Folha de São Paulo*/1996). The situation is so dramatic that many sectors which had never before been concerned about these issues began to discuss ways to ensure participation in the design and implementation of educational policy.

In the 1990s, when the stringent requirements of ISO 9000 and 14000 have made it difficult for Brazilian companies to sell their products on the international market, businesses have begun to show more interest in efforts to improve basic education. Entrepreneurs have taken a more critical approach toward education, which previously had been perceived as a high-risk investment.

It was in this context that Brazilian entrepreneurs entered into an agreement to produce a basic education program to be known as Telecurso 2000. This program was originally directed at the millions of young and adult workers who, for different reasons, had been denied the right to complete their basic education.

TELECURSO 2000 : PRODUCTION, USE AND EXPANSION

Telecurso 2000 is a condensed version of a basic curriculum for distance education which is to be provided through a combination of videotaped classroom sessions and books. Thus, both television sets and video cassette equipment are used. In addition, an optional curriculum is offered which focuses on teaching basic mechanical skills (the vocational course on mechanics).

The main factor that led the partnership between the FIESP System and the Roberto Marinho Foundation (FRM) to produce Telecurso 2000 was, without a doubt, the educational situation of Brazilian workers, which undermined the productivity of the Brazilian economy. Other variables also contributed to this undertaking, including the following: (1) the possibility of using the main television network in Brazil (GLOBO) as a vehicle for airing the program throughout the national territory, and (2) the existence of a universally accredited educational system, the supplementary education program, which was aimed specifically at people who were too old to attend regular schools. The certificates granted under this system are accepted and recognized everywhere in Brazil. The supplementary education program provides what might be termed "compensatory education." The Telecurso 2000 curriculum is structured as a form of supplementary education.

The initial discussions on the development of a curriculum for the three courses to be offered by Telecurso 2000 (Level One, Level Two and the Vocational Course on Mechanics) were subsidized by education specialists who wished to elucidate the teaching of basic skills in the context of a postindustrial society.

With that beginning, the guiding principles for the educational program of Telecurso 2000 were developed as follows:

1) *Job-oriented education*. The purpose is to educate individuals for a job: to educate workers so as to enable them to relate in a meaningful way to life in society, bearing in mind the fundamental role of education in ensuring worker productivity.

2) *Development of basic skills*. In a society marked by scientific and technological progress, it is not enough simply to learn to read, write, count and solve simple arithmetic and geometry problems. It is essential to enable people to organize their thoughts, to solve problems involving numbers, to interpret what they read and apply it in different situations, to read and express themselves in another language, to understand instruction manuals, to develop basic know-how in economics and quality control so as to be able to produce more and better products and eliminate waste, to hold discussions by making use of cognitive and social skills.

3) *Citizenship education*. The nature of the new relationship between science, technology and society makes it necessary for workers in all categories and at all levels to broaden the scope of their learning, so as to enable them to play an active role in the political and cultural scenes. Production-oriented skills must go hand-in-hand with civic responsibility.

4) *Contextualization*. The most advanced teaching practices stress the importance of applying what is learned in class to situations that arise in daily life. In other words, daily life provides the material for the teaching of specific skills.

These four principles—job-oriented education, development of basic skills, citizenship education and contextualization—underlie all the disciplines that are taught through Telecurso 2000. The development of the program content for each discipline was entrusted to teams of professors associated with the major universities, all of whom were required to have ample experience in the field of basic education. This requirement was particularly important given the highly specialized nature of adult education and the need to adjust the language to be used accordingly. Textbooks had to be easy to read without being childish.

The following table shows the content of the curricula for the three courses offered by Telecurso 2000, as well as the number of TV classrooms and books used in each discipline.

Typically, the process of producing the different courses and disciplines included in Telecurso 2000 has followed these stages: once the general curriculum was outlined, specific curricula were developed for each discipline. These in turn guided the teams of professors in writing

Table 1. Composition and resources of Telecurso 2000.

Course	Discipline	TV Sessions N	TV Sessions Hours	Resource Video	Resource Books	Hours of study required
Level 1	Math	80	20.0	10	4	
	Portuguese	90	22.5	12	4	
	Brazilian History	40	10.0	5	2	1 hour 45 minutes
	Geography	50	12.5	7	2	per class
	Science	70	17.5	9	3	session
	English	30	7.5	4	1	
Total	**6**	**360**	**90.0**	**47**	**16**	**630 hours**
Level 2	Math	70	17.5	9	3	
	Portuguese	80	20.0	10	3	
	Chemistry	50	12.5	7	2	
	Physics	50	12.5	7	2	1 hours 45 minutes
	English	40	10.0	5	2	per class
	Biology 50	12.5	7	2		session
	Brazilian History	80	20.0	10	4	
	Gen. Geography	40	10.0	5	2	
Total	**8**	**460**	**115.0**	**60**	**20**	**735 hours**
Technical Course on Mechanics	17 modules including a variety of subjects	360	90.0	53	19	1 hours 45 minutes per class session= 630 hours

the textbooks for each class, and exercises and suggested classroom procedures were then developed on the basis of the textbooks. These suggestions were then submitted to communications specialists who were responsible for "marrying" the formal educational content with the informal language of television. At all stages of the process, evaluations were conducted which included the reading of materials by internal (FRM) and external (contract) specialists called "critical readers." Thus, each discipline/course went through many steps—backwards and forwards — until a final approved version was ready.

Learning in the context of Telecurso 2000 takes place in three distinct ways, as follows:

1) *Individual learning.* This entails learning the cognitive-affective skills required for individual study and reading with comprehension.

2) *Classroom instruction.* This presupposes the existence of a "tele-classroom" (classroom with a TV set and VCR equipment) in a public

or private institution, where a facilitator encourages learning. In this dimension, the group is predominant; this means that mutual cooperation is a vital part of the collective construction of knowledge.

3) *Informal mentoring.* This is provided by learning facilitators in a facility equipped with TV and VCR.

In any of these dimensions, when students feel they are ready, they may take the supplementary education tests offered by the different states of Brazil (through their Secretariats of Education). Students must pass a test for each discipline, as in a credit system. When students have passed all the disciplines included in a study program, they receive a certificate which is valid anywhere in the national territory.

In order to extend Telecurso 2000 throughout the country, the producers have entered into agreements (in the case of major institutions, such as universities, state and municipal Secretariats of Education, ministries, foundations, non-governmental organizations) and terms of participation (with corporations and individual entities). This has made it possible to open a large number of teleclassrooms (4,000 at this writing), with a regular attendance of 110,000 "telestudents."

Thanks to these strategies, Telecurso 2000 (which was launched on 2 January 1995) has become well known throughout the country, and has opened up new opportunities for adults to "go back to school" and earn certificates at both levels of basic education.

The Internet and Intranets for Education and Training

A Framework for action by Latin America and the Caribean

T he Internet and intranets will form the backbone of the knowledge economy in the 21st Century, and will both enable and require new models of education and training. Investment in new educational models and infrastructures to support these models is criti-

Linda M. Harasim

cal. It is especially urgent in Latin America and the Caribbean, where strategic investments in education and training can contribute to significant economic and social benefits today and the potential to thrive in the new global knowledge economies tomorrow. The challenge is to ready millions of people to become knowledge workers in these global economies. Education and training must be knowledge based, and strategies to develop and implement them must

Dr. Harasim is leader and CEO of the TeleLearning Network of Centers of Excellence at the Simon Fraser University, Burnaby, B.C., Canada.

incorporate special educational environments on the Internet and World Wide Web that are specially customized to support knowledge work and collaborative learning. The development of multi-level partnerships among networks of centers of excellence for research and development and the building of distributed cores of expertise and practice (distributed in geography and specialization) for social and economic purposes will be key to strategic development.

INTRODUCTION

This paper considers the current and potential role of the Internet and its private organizational counterparts, intranets, for education and training in Latin America and the Caribbean. Today we are at a social crossroads unlike any in the history of human civilization. The convergence of powerful computers with telecommunications technologies over the past three decades is precipitating a profound social and economic transformation that will have an impact on all countries in the world, unequally. Some countries may experience very positive results while others will experience negative outcomes. The outcomes, however, are not predestined; impacts will be significantly determined by national and local policy and investment. In education and training, strategic investment in technological infrastructure will be essential but not sufficient conditions to achieve success. Investment in advanced educational models, in specially customized educational network technologies, and in retraining educators to effectively implement these new educational approaches is even more essential.

This is thus a pivotal time in human history and development: Unlike previous major socioeconomic shifts, the current paradigm shift can be influenced by decisions which can shape, to a significant degree, the outcomes. Such investments, moreover, will yield high dividends in both the short and long term, by providing a launching pad and an infrastructure for building the future. For developing nations, strategic planning and investments in education and training are especially urgent measures to survive, and potentially to thrive, by leapfrogging into advanced educational networking. They are also essential to maintaining national intellectual sovereignty.

Throughout human history, technology breakthroughs and new social forms have combined, each influencing the other, to create new ways of life that spread throughout the human species (Keating and Mustard, 1993). Thus, the concept of 'paradigm shift' is not simply a product of popular media. There are serious issues and challenges that require research, planning, preparation and investment. Network technologies both require and enable new forms of education and training. A crude chronology of previous major shifts would include the Agricultural Revolution (10,000 BC), the Industrial Revolution (1700 AD), and the Knowledge Revolution of 2000 AD. We can look back and see what was. We can also look ahead and anticipate what might be.

Here is one scenario that could be envisaged:

2000 A.D.: Advanced information technology interacts with powerful new models of education and training to produce knowledge-based economies and the democratization of knowledge production. Countries in Latin America and the Caribbean have invested in powerful national networks linked to the Internet and intranets enabling their citizens to access essential services related to education, training, health, and many other areas. All children become fully educated, and adults have access to ongoing professional development, just-in-time training, and lifelong learning. Geographic location does not determine whether the information highway passes one's door. Latin America and the Caribbean have invested in the infrastructure and know-how to build learning societies and develop knowledge industries that create the basis for economic well-being and democratize social benefits for the population. The citizens become not just consumers of new knowledge services but active producers and providers of knowledge work and industries that form part of a global network.

An alternative scenario is equally possible:

2000 A.D.: Advanced information technology interacts with a widening split between educationally advantaged and disadvantaged groups, leading to a new kind of caste system and to the rapid decline of nations unable to keep up with the ever-increasing demand for knowledge and skills. Differences in access to the Information Highway exacerbate two-tiered societies, increasing gaps between haves and have-nots, knowers and know-nots, men and women, north and south, whites and other races, skilled professionals and unskilled hourly workers. Nations in Latin America and the Caribbean without skilled human resources and technological infrastructure are unable to develop knowledge industries and cannot participate in the global knowledge economy. There is widespread poverty, unemployment is at record levels and rising, social hardship is profound, and public unrest is mounting as the economy spirals ever downward and basic needs are increasingly unmet at a national level. There is little hope for improvement or remedial action given that skilled labor and know-how are not available. The last-minute investment in technological infrastructure proves futile.

Education is key to determining which of the above scenarios proves the more accurate. Valuable lessons generated through a significant history of two decades of field practice and research in learning networks are available to guide effective national strategies and investment.

How are networks used for education?

The concept of "Internet" refers to a vast network of interconnected computer networks that enables computers of all platforms to share services and communicate directly. The Internet refers to the public network, while intranets are *private* networks, with gateways to the Internet accessible only by members of that organization. The Internet is a progeny of the first computer network in the world, the ARPANET, which was inspired by the need to share resources, to facilitate human communication and interaction, and to augment human intellect through distributed collaboration (Hafner and Lyon, 1996). This vision is being fulfilled by educational applications of networking.

The ARPANET began in 1969, and electronic mail over distributed networks was invented in 1971. Educational applications of computer networks followed almost immediately. By the mid-1970s, academics began to use computer networks to augment educational activities in their university classrooms and network learning began. The term "network learning" (as well as on-line education and training) will be used henceforth to refer to educational applications of the Internet and intranets. Network learning was soon adopted by public educators (1981), corporate education programs (1981), public schools for classroom networking (1983), and universities for on-line course delivery (1984).

An overview of on-line education and training indicates that the Internet and intranets can be employed in one of three modes: *adjunct mode*; mixed mode; and totally on-line mode. In adjunct mode, networks are used to enhance regular classrooms and distance education. The major applications involve enriching classroom activities by using networks for class discussions; extending office hours for Q&A; assignment submissions; enabling class collaboration and team projects; enhancing group knowledge, work, and analysis; and expanding access to communities of learners, practitioners, experts, and research resources. Networked classroom approaches (linking classes in different disciplines and/or countries), TeleApprenticeship, Ask an Expert and Electronic Field Trips are examples of adjunct mode applications. In *mixed mode,* a significant portion of the educational activity occurs on-line, while the remainder occurs in traditional mode of face-to-face classrooms or distance education. The applications include professional development programs, continuing education, training, credit courses, and labs. In *totally on-line mode*, all education or training activity is conducted on-line. Examples include on-line courses, on-line degree or diploma courses, on-line mini-courses, special interest courses, and just-in-time training.

LESSONS TO DATE: WHAT HAS PROVEN USABLE AND SUCCESSFUL?

Important lessons to guide this new field have been generated by the first two decades of research and educational use of the Internet. New models and approaches to education and training have resulted.

The most critical issue is wiring schools to what and to whom. Wiring educational and training institutions, albeit a major challenge, is minor compared to the more fundamental issue: the need to identify proven, effective and appropriate applications. Equally urgent is the need to help educators and trainers adopt, implement and assess these applications effectively. Nonetheless, educators, learners, and researchers agree that the results are worthwhile.

Lesson 1: Network learning is effective. The major lesson is that learning networks do work and generate positive impacts at all levels of education: primary, secondary, tertiary and adult education. This statement summarizes two decades of field experimentation and research. Researchers have found that network learning can enhance and expand the traditional ways of teaching and learning, both in classroom teaching and at a distance. Perhaps more importantly, it can effectively offer entirely new opportunities for learning.

Lesson 2: Educational design is key. In order to work well, however, educators must attend to principled design: design of both new pedagogies and environments that support effective learning. Principled design — that is, design based on advanced educational principles such as support for active collaborative learning, equitable access, multiple perspectives, and knowledge building—holds significant potential for improving learning. There are five core principles:

Principle of Collaboration: The principle of collaboration involves the engagement of learners in cooperative rather than competitive pursuit of knowledge. Collaborative learning involves a change in the role of the instructor from that of authority and chief source of information (sage on the stage) to facilitator and resource support (guide on the side).

Principle of Access: Effective educational applications of the Internet must promote access, including geographic access (especially by rural as well as urban populations); temporal access (24 hour/day, 7 days/week); and equitable access (transcending gender, age, racial, physical or socioeconomic barriers).

Principle of Active Learning: Learning is enhanced by active articulation and organizing of ideas and information into knowledge structures. Learners need opportunities to participate and present-debate-develop-refine ideas in and through a forum.

Principle of Multiple Perspectives: Knowledge is complex, dynamic, and context sensitive. Instruction should promote multiple perspectives, representations, and strategies.

Principle of Knowledge Work: Learners actively construct knowledge by formulating ideas into words and representations. These ideas are built upon through the reactions of others to the formulation. Real world problem solving demands engagement, self-direction, goal setting, inquiry, reasoning and reflecting.

Lesson 3: Customize Internet environments for education and training, with special tools and supports for teachers and learners. Just as physical space has been customized for specific applications (classrooms, cafeterias, boardrooms, seminar rooms, offices, etc.), so too must virtual space on the Internet be customized to best support specific applications and activities. This customization must also be based on principled design (see lesson 2 above) and tailored by principled development of specialized educational tools and scaffolds.

Lesson 4: Network learning offers a conceptual and technological framework for lifelong learning. Network learning should be viewed as part of a larger strategy, to reform/rethink education, establish learning communities and contribute to building a knowledge economy and learning society.

Lesson 5: Network learning provides and requires new research opportunities and research methodologies to expand our study and appreciation of knowledge work, learning sciences, and conceptual change.

Lesson 6: Pilot projects in education and training, involving public-private partnerships and the use of information technology, are proliferating in Europe, Asia, the U.S.A. and Canada. These can provide a source for benchmarks of best practices to ensure wider diffusion.

Some examples

The Internet is used at all levels of education, including public schools, post-secondary institutions, training, corporate education and continuing professional education. Below are examples from Canada, Europe, and the U.S.

Networked classrooms and schools

Primary and secondary schools and classrooms around the world have since the early 1980s used networks to link with one another for collaborative projects, access to experts or communities of practice, access to resources and to peer networking (Harasim et al, 1995) . Most networks are free, funded through public support or governmental funds; others are commercial and link through intranets. Some highly regarded public examples include the **US National Geographic Kids Network,** working with TERC to encourage students to conduct original research into topics of scientific, geographic and social significance; the **Writers in Electronic Residence** program in Canada, which links writing and language arts students with well-known writers, teachers and one another in a form of "teleapprenticeship"; **WebCSILE**, a collaborative database and knowledge building environment being used in the U.S., Canada (including the north), Europe and Australia; and National Science Foundation projects such as the **National School Network** and CoVIS. (Web URL addresses of these and additional sites appear in the Appendix.) Teachers also use networking for professional development and professional support environments (for example, **FrEdNet** in the U.S.A. and the **Educators' Network of Ontario** in Canada). All the above examples used the Internet in adjunct mode. In cases of home schooling and in small remote communities, the Internet may be used for mixed mode or totally on-line mode course delivery.

School and community initiatives

The Internet is also used to support school and community initiatives. **Sister Cities** focuses on citizen diplomacy in the United States, and globally with local community development and volunteer action programs in 1,200 U.S. cities and their 1,900 partners in 120 countries worldwide. Active since the late 1980s, **I*EARN**, the International Education and Resource Network enables young people to undertake projects designed to make a contribution to the health and welfare of the planet and its people. I*EARN is international, with member schools in over 30 countries, supporting students and teachers in collaborative projects to make a meaningful difference in the world as part of the educational process.

University level offerings

In the mid-1970s universities began using networks, mostly in adjunct mode. Since 1984, beginning with the Virtual Classroom undergraduate project at New Jersey Institute for Technology (Hiltz,1994) university and college courses began offering courses entirely on-line and in mixed mode. University use of the Internet is increasingly common, but is primarily still the result of individual initiatives rather than faculty or university-wide programming.

The Open University in the U.K. began using networks to enhance traditional distance education activities in 1989, and this initiative has grown with many courses now being offered totally on-line. In addition, it is now experimenting with **RealAudio** to deliver real time lectures on a global scale, using its own interface for this purpose entitled **KMI Stadium** which also provides facilities for slides associated with the lecture. In 1985, the Ontario Institute for Studies in Education/ University of Toronto was the first to offer graduate courses entirely on-line (Harasim et al, 1995), and today OISE continues to offer many on-line courses. Simon Fraser University began using networks in mixed mode in 1990 and, with the development of the **Virtual-U** (see below), now offers a large number of courses in mixed or on-line mode. SFU also offers degree and diploma programs on-line. Canada's **Acadia University** plans to be the first fully electronic campus in Canada, having chosen the "ThinkPad University" approach to integrate computers into the teaching and learning environment and to equip every student, by the year 2000, with an IBM ThinkPad notebook computer. In the fall of 1997, all first-year, full-time students will be issued an IBM ThinkPad as part of their tuition, as well as instruction on how to use the notebook inside and outside the classroom.

A new phenomenon is that of the totally on-line university or training program. Mason (1997) notes however that many of these initiatives are based on "cyberspeak." "These are the virtual universities, designed for a global platform and operating purely electronically. Some are idealistic and visionary in aim, such as the **Globewide Network Academy** and **Spectrum Virtual University**. Others are 'for profit,' such as **Phoenix University** and **IMLearn**. The scale of these operations is variable: many of them on investigation prove to be working from one office; others have significant numbers (e.g. 2000 registered for on-line courses at Phoenix University), although very few students will be non-nationals." Mason notes that "these are not universities in the commonly accepted sense of the term: they borrow academics from other institutions rather than fund their own established full-time faculty; they do not cover a full range of discipline areas; they do not fund research programs and they do not support what is usually called an academic environment. Nevertheless, they provide courses which people want; they are capitalizing on the phenomenal growth of the Internet and are trail-blazing the global pathways for others (p. 15-16)."

Business providers of university education, continuing education & workplace training

A new entrant to the field of educational delivery is the business which becomes an educational provider. Mason (1997) reports that "This group consists of organizations whose primary business is not, or has not been, education. Often they have services or products which have now become central to the delivery of global education. The obvious examples are telecommunications providers, whether satellites, cable, telephone or combinations. Other examples come from the computer and software industries. The advent of these new providers offering professional updating programs, adult education courses, life-long learning opportunities and just-in-time training resources to what has always been the market monopolized by universities and continuing education units, has caused ripples of alarm in all but the most unreconstructed universities (p. 16)." Examples include:

- **Knowledge On-line** by U.S.-based Jones Education Company. Through their "Jones College Connection" site, they offer both courses and degree programs from U.S. universities delivered to the home or office by cable technologies and some use of the Internet.

- **IBM Global Network** enables colleges and universities to re-engineer learning and teaching through design, development, delivery, and management of distributed learning. Some initial features include Lotus LearningSpace, a Notes-based environment for team-based learning, teaching, and student support; IBM Digital Library, for archiving large amounts of data electronically; IBM Internet Connection, for dial-up network and Internet access; and an on-line catalog.

- **Microsoft On-line Institute** (MOLI) is a 'virtual' university campus that offers courses on Microsoft products and can be accessed via the Internet. MOLI provides an alternative to classroom training allowing the student to study whenever or wherever they like. MOLI courses can be joined at any time and last for a number of weeks. The student enrolls on a class and then works through self paced courseware at home or work, engaging with an on-line tutor via e-mail, bulletin boards and chats.

- **Stanford Professional Development Center: Stanford On-line** provides technology professionals at industry sites worldwide a wide range of continuing engineering education options in a variety of formats including broadcast, instructional modules, executive education, and customized courseware. The Stanford On-line project of SPDC makes Stanford engineering and computer science courses available anywhere, anytime on demand, using video with audio, text, and graphics.

- **Motorola University** began in 1981 as the Motorola Training and Education center. It was created as a result of an analysis of Motorola's training needs and established as a corporate department in the human resources function. Since 1990, Motorola University had diversified further, establishing academic partnerships with institutes of higher learning around the world. Motorola University has also implemented cultural design and translation services. This has become especially important as Motorola moves into new and emerging markets in Eastern Europe, South America and the Asia-Pacific region. The University's instructional design and development efforts are divided into competency centers.

- **CAL Campus** is a private, international distance education and training center based in New York on the concept of a community college, which offers courses through the Internet. Most courses are Directed Independent Study, which are designed so that students receive lessons from their teachers through the Internet to study off-line. Course materials come in the forms of all-in-one disk-texts that are run on a computer, text lessons that are downloaded and printed, or in some cases a hard-copy textbook. Students are required to do homework assignments and quizzes which are e-mailed to their CALC instructors for evaluation.

New software environments based on advanced educational principles: Virtual-U

All of the above examples use the Internet for educational delivery or enhancement, but do not provide a customized on-line learning environment. Rather, most use generic computer and networking tools which instructors then try to shape into effective environments. While this is certainly possible and is the way in which many of us began, it is very difficult and the chances of success in creating effective learning are reduced. Without the necessary educational tools and supports, educators and learners will either fail, give up or require significant effort and motivation to transform a generic system into an educational classroom, seminar, or lab.

Virtual-U is software specially customized to enable the creation and use of on-line learning environments. Based on fifteen years of research and field experience, Virtual-U is one of the first in the world to develop an environment customized to support educators and learners to be successful, more easily, in on-line education and training. Virtual-U is used by schools, universities, government agencies, and workplaces in a wide variety of disciplines around the world.

Using the Virtual-U software, educators put their courses on the Web. Virtual-U provides tools to easily create and upload course material, to set up on-line (asynchronous) discussion groups and project teams, and to support problem solving and knowledge work. Using interactive discourse as a pedagogic strategy, Virtual-U provides the framework for conducting collaborative educational projects and knowledge-based discussions. The activities may include on-line debates, role plays, moderating and participating in discussions or seminars, coordinating project activities, analyzing and presenting project results, and so on. These types of group-based experiences can provide the structure for the social construction of knowledge, one of the primary goals of Virtual-U's designers and developers.

Because Virtual-U operates in the Web's hyper-linked environment, direct links to course activities and resources or to information at other sites on the Web can be included in the course materials. Virtual-U also integrates a grade book tool. The teacher can use this grade book tool to automatically calculate student averages and display bar charts comparing any given student's performance to the rest of the class's aggregate performance. Students can check their own individual grades (but not those of other students) at any time.

A few words on institutional strategies for using Virtual-U. Many institutions are struggling with the issues of cost, access and quality of instruction. Research demonstrates that with careful planning and design, networking technology can make valuable contributions in all these areas. However, there is no single model for increasing access to education, reducing the cost and improving the quality of the learning experience.

Institutions are using Virtual-U in a variety of ways. Some institutions have purchased and installed Virtual-U to deliver totally on-line course offerings in such subject areas as dance and the performing arts, computer science, engineering science, literature, education, medicine, communication, and business. Degree and diploma programs in such areas as graduate nursing and MBA studies are also offered via Virtual-U. An International Labor Studies program is also being offered on-line by a group of public unions. Other schools use Virtual-U to provide new options and more interactivity for campus-based courses. These "mixed mode" courses involve some face-to-face class sessions with the instructor as well as Virtual-U's on-line discussions to cover topics in more depth than can be pursued in the typical class meeting.

This form of learning experience is more than using e-mail to communicate with students. It involves a new role for the teacher. The role of designing the learning environment for students is more like that of a facilitator, guide or mentor. The actual "construction of knowledge" is done by students themselves within the on-line discussions as they explore different perspectives on issues, contrast potential solutions, or offer insights based on their own research. Sometimes the teacher will moderate these discussions, sometimes a student or a team of students moderates. An important part of the process is that students are acquiring new learning and communications skills in the process of creating knowledge. They are learning to collaborate as a group and work as a team to find, process and analyze information.

The student now has multiple opportunities for interaction: with the instructor, with other students in the course, with peers, practitioners and experts globally, and with the information itself. In addition, the students effectively have 24 hours a day, 7 days a week to participate because asynchronous conferencing does not take place in "real time."

Regional or national initiatives

Several noteworthy state or national programs have been launched to promote a coordinated effort in network learning. One U.S. example receiving significant media attention is the **Western Governors' Initiative**. Still primarily in the planning stage, it is charged with creating a design plan for a western virtual university to serve the region and an implementation plan through which such an entity could be established and financed. The goals of the initiative include: expanding access to a broader range of post-secondary education opportunities; reducing costs providing a vehicle for cost sharing; providing a means for learners to obtain formal recognition of the skills and knowledge they have acquired through advanced technology-based learning outside the formal educational system; creating high performance standards; and demonstrating new approaches to teaching and assessment.

While the Western Governor's Initiative is largely programmatic, the **Canadian School Net** exemplifies a national strategy for providing the technological infrastructure as well as pedagogical supports for the use of the Internet in education and training, suggesting a valuable example for countries in Latin America and the Caribbean. Canada's SchoolNet is a collaborative initiative designed to facilitate the effective use of information technology and foster the development of employability skills required to compete in the knowledge-based economy. SchoolNet's goal is to facilitate access by all of Canada's 16,500 schools, 450 First Nations schools, 3,400 public libraries, and rural communities to the information highway by 1999.

SchoolNet is an alliance of public and private sector partners including provincial ministries of education, education and telecommunication associations and companies, research and development agencies and academia. Through these partnerships, SchoolNet is promoting the development of Canadian-produced multimedia educational resources and ensuring that the learning opportunities presented by the information highway are equally accessible to all Canadians. Through the guidance of an advisory board and network coalition, SchoolNet helps to facilitate excellence in learning through electronic networking across Canada and helping to move learning from being teacher centered to learner-community centered.

LESSONS TO DATE: WHAT HASN'T WORKED?

The past decades of field practice and educational research in use of the Internet also have yielded valuable lessons on what does not work well or work at all. Here follow examples of common implementation mistakes that education and training institutions make when trying to reinvent themselves on the Internet. The examples are drawn from U.S., Canadian and European cases. The first nine examples are drawn from Bacsich (1997).

- In Europe there are many good research projects; nonetheless many are disconnected from the market and commercial developers (most of whom are on the U.S. West Coast).

- There is a great need for trainer training. But often the trainers are trained by those who lack serious experience with the technologies in education. This may work with video conferencing, but computer conferencing and Web use in education have sufficient subtlety that this trickle-down process does not lead to good results.

- There is still a great deal of "reinventing the wheel" both technically and educationally. For example, the European Commission has on more than one occasion identified lack of dissemination as a problem, with a mild rebuke to the disseminators; but as Chairman of a dissemination organization, Bacsich notes from his own experience how hard it is to disseminate to those who do not want to be disseminated to.

- There is no one in charge: either there is a battle between sectors or there is inadequate institutional support.

- There is no succession plan for replacing current leadership.

- R&D replaces implementation. This is a classic problem when researchers are put in charge. Researchers always have reasons that seem good to them for not adopting what has worked before. Yet on the other hand there are dangers if non-researchers are put in charge—they may not be adequately informed, even with current technologies.

- The adoption/roll-out "jump" is badly done. After the researchers have developed a system, they tend to lose interest and want to move to the next challenge. Yet for the system to be successful, some agency has to roll it out; for example the Computing Service. The potential for misunderstanding (at best) and power politics (at worst) is enormous.

- The periphery fights the center. This is common in multi-campus institutions.

- An old-fashioned unit gains control. In the U.K., forces centered on the Library often come out in charge of educational technology. In some cases that works well, when the Library has re-invented itself; in other cases it merely holds things back. In Canada and the U.S. it is common for a re-invented Computing Service to gain control. This can work; but it can also fail.

There are also many other problems or failures:

- A software is chosen because of a perceived bargain price (without regard for the very high expense of training educators who then reject it or find it is inappropriate) or because of fancy features and glitz rather than usability factors.

- A researcher is given the lead on a large course.Unfortunately, he wanted to develop a new system rather than use existing (and adequate) technology. Students are still waiting for the course to come out. See the next point.

- The institution decides "We can build it ourselves," and tries to reinvent the entire software system without adequately appreciating the costs involved, the need to base the technology on educational models, the risk of doing it poorly, or the need for extensive field testing. The results are either vaporware, or an inadequate system that students and teachers ultimately reject. Significant user good will and faith in network learning as well as valuable time are lost, and the institution is unable to regain its initiatives in this area.

- Activities are launched as projects rather than institutional or national programs. Either the results are haphazard or a form of Balkanization ensues, since different departments or schools use different (incompatible) systems and partnerships are foiled.

- State and provincial governments launch "learning networks" but focus on wiring schools without a strategic vision that considers learning activities, teacher training, or assessment protocols.

- Large programs are launched on the Internet using old paradigm models, based on traditional distance education or video conferencing (transmission mode) rather than investing in educational models that support new paradigm activities of knowledge work. The result is that learners do not gain requisite analytical or problem-solving skills or scientific mindsets for the new economy.

- In Canada and the U.S., some universities have pronounced their commitment to be fully on-line, or to integrate the Internet into all aspects of instruction. Despite the bold move on the part of university administration and ongoing pressure from students to change instructional approaches, the universities are beleaguered by the lack of a vision. There is no plan regarding which learning models and approaches are effective and should be used, or how to educate and retrain faculty in appropriate use and assessment of new instructional approaches.

- There are inadequate linkages among researchers or between advanced research and practitioners. For example, the U.S. National Science Foundation provides major funding for advanced educational research projects. There are few mechanisms to encourage linkages and sharing among the various research projects, or between researchers and practitioners.

- "Edutainment" wins out over powerful educational models, and the learners do not develop the strong analytical and innovative abilities necessary to find jobs or to build knowledge industries.

- Expectations are unrealistic; technology is viewed as a panacea rather than as an environment that with good educational design can support powerful learning processes.

NEW DIRECTIONS: WHAT IS PROMISING?

Despite pitfalls such as these, promising developments have emerged in the pursuit of strategies to tackle the monumental education and training challenges that face societies globally. These deserve further exploration, development and refinement, through investment and expansion, in order to yield the high level dividends promised.

There is a pressing need to build on earlier successes. The lessons to date, as represented in the examples on previous pages, came from important initiatives, but for the most part these initiatives can be characterized as small, one-of-a-kind or independent: efforts by individual educators, schools, institutions, or independent programs. What is required now is to link, leverage, integrate and advance the most promising activities into a strategic initiative or set of initiatives, in order to test and disseminate the results.

There is a need to focus on models of learning that best support and advance new paradigms of learning, based on knowledge work; there is a need to develop network environments for education and training that are especially customized to support collaborative learning and knowledge work; and there is a need for implementation strategies that include ongoing teacher training and assessment. Partnerships between researchers and practitioners, between educational researchers and technology builders, and among the academy, public and private sectors are key to developing networks of centers of excellence and distributed cores of expertise.

The TeleLearning Network of Centers of Excellence (TL•NCE) is a unique model worldwide in that it is a nation-wide initiative, committed to pursuing such goals. It does so with a powerful strategy based on networking the best scientific and academic talent in Canada with government, public and private sector leaders who are also committed to advancing education and training.

This program has addressed the following key issues:

- Strategic planning for readying learners for the knowledge-based economy and the globalization of the workplace

- Effective partnerships among academic/governmental/private sectors

- Design and testing of new pedagogies and on-line environments

- Integrating new pedagogies/instructional models and assessment

- Commercializing research and building knowledge industries

- Consistency of product development and quality control and need to establish standards

- Supporting the changing role of the educators, trainers and educational administration

- Fostering the development of national, regional and global, multilingual and multicultural resources

- Developing on-line environments that support advanced educational approaches, using exponentially available bandwidth (i.e., Internet 2) effectively and appropriately

- Developing distributed cores: creating regional and global alliances and partnerships that build on best local expertise and link with needed competencies in other parts of the country/world

RECOMMENDATIONS

This paper has examined how the Internet and its private organizational counterparts, intranets, are used in education and training. The key lessons identified can, with country and region specification, contribute to building a framework for action for the countries of Latin America and the Caribbean. Timing is both a challenge and an opportunity. Economic globalization and networking advances create an urgency for new models of education and training. At the same time, valuable lessons have already been learned in other countries that can help Latin America and the Caribbean avoid costly mistakes, and assist in identifying the proven successes that can inform national and regional strategies for major educational advances and leapfrogging.

Key lessons are the need to develop educational strategies that are knowledge based, based on new-paradigm educational principles.

These strategies are not technology-driven but technology-enabled, and include knowledge work models of learning, instructional and assessment approaches, teacher training, and especially knowledge-based design and customization of network learning environments. The idea is not to reinvent the wheel but to build on the successes of others in network learning and to form partnerships, both locally and globally, with strategic stakeholders. These stakeholders include researchers, developers, and client communities. The goal of the partnerships is to leverage the best and make the most of scarce resources. Finally, standardization of common platforms and software environments should be considered.

Recommendations for national programs

1. Create a national strategy to:

● Build preparedness of all the country's human resources

● Develop criteria to address the key education issue: "wiring for what and with whom?" National targets should be set not just for wiring/connectivity but for educational goals.

● Develop a connectivity plan: forecast which technologies will be available for education and when. Ensure uniformity in telecommunications investment, so that the gap between urban and rural areas is not increased, but decreased. Broadband is not necessary for many effective education and training applications. If the telecommunications industry is unwilling or unable to wire the rural areas, investigate wireless communication options.

2. Create distributed national and regional research sites and exemplary models/sites which will:

● Study and model effective applications

● Identify and support specific local/regional expertise for regional and global markets

3. Involve all stakeholders/players in a national coordinated effort to:

● Create national networks of centers of excellence in relevant areas

- Network teachers, trainers and students in classrooms and high end labs, homes and workplaces

- Create consortia of academic, public and private organizations for research and technology and content development

- Consider the use of common software, customized and tailored with modularization

- Develop virtual university and virtual schooling policies

4. Partner locally, nationally, and globally to:

- Connect local and national centers with International Networks of Centers of Excellence

- Undertake international scans of models and study what is appropriate to own situation

- Encourage knowledge networking, to leverage social and economic resources: linking schools, universities, science centers, museums, health and medical centers, etc.

- Standardization: consider national strategy that rolls out common software environments for public and/or post-secondary institutions. A common systems approach would offer benefits to users (the ability to establish support communities), advantages for training, familiarity for users, and the incentive of a common platform for content developers.

Recommendations for subregions, Latin America and the Caribbean

1. Establish exemplary schools and research centers whose role is to:

- Serve as a demonstration and showcase site on the use of network learning for national and international visitors

- Act as a center of excellence in the development of innovative uses of information technology in learning and content development, including working with national and regional structures to develop sophisticated on-line learning products, multimedia learning materials and digitization projects

Recommendations for NAFTA

1. Establish international networks of centers of excellence in order to:

- Establish hallmarks of learning: quality, flexibility, innovation, knowledge work

- Address common challenges: access, new skills and mindsets, leverage resources by local and global partnerships

- Build strategy: provide incentives, infrastructure, information, and global perspectives

- Encourage research and training standards

2. Partner.
Partnerships with national and other NCEs, such as Canada's TeleLearning Network of Centers of Excellence, the U.S. National Science Foundation projects, and institutional innovators in Mexico (Universidad Virtual), offer the most promising route toward promoting and achieving world-class research, technology development, content development, and alliances with funding institutions. Membership in an International Network of Centers of Excellence in TeleLearning (INCET) could support translation of telelearning R&D into practice, through programs to support technology transfer, re-education of educators and trainers, and the development of appropriate assessment and monitoring protocols and practice.

3. Global export/import opportunities.
Opportunities for global export and import are central to a strategic and coordinated view of investment in on-line education and training. Development and participation in Distributed Cores of Expertise and International Networks of Centers of Excellence in TeleLearning are key, supporting strategic partnerships between producers and client communities. The client community consists of companies who design, develop and market the technical systems, as well as the user communities (schools, universities and colleges, and workplace training organizations). The partners in the client community need to collaborate with university researchers to conceptualize, design , implement and evaluate prototype systems that can then be commercialized. There is a major global market for telelearning and teletraining knowhow, content, and technological infrastructures.

References, Resources and Web Sites

REFERENCES

Knight (pages 48-57)

Australian Qualifications Framework Advisory Board Secretariat (n.d.).

Australian Qualifications Framework.
http://www.curriculum.edu.au/aqfab.htm

Castro, Claudio Moura (1997). "Education in the Information Age: Promises and Frustrations." Paper prepared for the Forum on Education in the Information Age, Cartagena, Colombia, 9-11 July 1997.

Conte, Christopher (1997). The Learning Connection: Schools in the Information Age. Washington, D.C, The Benton Foundation, Communications Policy and Practice Program, What's Going On series.

Daniel, Sir John (1996). Mega-Universities and Knowledge Media: Technology Strategies for Higher Education. London, Kogan Page.

Daniel, Sir John (with Anne Stevens) (1997). "The Success Stories: the Use of Technology in 'Out-of-School' Education." Paper prepared for the Forum on Education in the Information Age, Cartagena, Colombia, 9-11 July 1997.

Fundação Roberto Marinho (n.d.). Website.
http://www.frm.org.br/tc2000/

Harasim, Linda (1997). "The Internet and Intranets for Education and
Training: A Framework for Action by Latin America and the
Caribbean." Paper prepared for the Forum on Education in the
Information Age, Cartagena, Colombia, 9-11 July 1997.
Kazachkov, Mikhail, Peter T. Knight and Brian Regli (1996). "Using
Distance Learning to Facilitate the Transformation of the Regulatory,
Business, and Social Environment in Russia." Paper prepared for the
Second International Conference on Distance Education in Russia, 2-5
July 1996, Moscow, Russian Federation. http://www.knight-
moore.com/html/transformation_in_russia.html

Knight, Peter T. (1995). "The Telematics Revolution in Africa and the
World Bank Role".http://www.knight-
moore.com/html/telematics_in_africa.html

Knight, Peter T. (1996). "Destined to Leapfrog: Why a Revolution in
Learning will Occur in Brazil, Russia, and South Africa". Paper prepared for the Second International Conference on Distance Education
in Russia, 2-5 July 1996, Moscow, Russian Federation.
http://www.knight-moore.com/html/leapfrog.html

Moore, Michael G. and Kearsley, Greg (1996). Distance Education: A
Systems View. Belmont, California: Wadsworth Publishing Company.

New Zeland Qualifications Authority (n.d.). Website.
http://www.nzqa.govt.nz/

Oliveira, João Batista Araujo e, 1997. "Distance Learning &
Technology in Brazil." Paper prepared for the Forum on Education in
the Information Age, Cartagena, Colombia, 9-11 July 1997.

Rectoria de la Universidad Virtual (n.d.). Website.
http://www.ruv.itesm.mx/

Schumpeter, Joseph A. (1942). Capitalism, Socialism, and Democracy.
New York: Harper Brothers. (Republished in Harper Torchbooks,
1976).

United Nations Economic Commission for Africa, 1996. African Information Society Initiative (AISI): an Action Framework to Build Africa's Information and Communication Infrastructure. http://www.bellanet.org/partners/aisi

Romizowski (pages 58-73)

Chang, E. (1994). Investigation of constructivist principles applied to collaborative study of business cases in computer-mediated communication. Unpublished doctoral dissertation, Syracuse University, Syracuse, New York.

Chute, A.G., et al. (1988). Learning from teletraining. American Journal of Distance Education, 2(3), 55-63.

Chute, A.G., et al. (1990). Strategies for implementing teletraining systems.Educational & Training Technology International, 27(3), 264-70.

Cunningham, D.J., Duffy, T.M. & Knuth, R.A. (1993). The textbook of the future. In C. McKnight (ed.), Hypertext: a psychological perspective. London: Horwood.

Dills, C.R., & Romiszowski, A.J. (1997). Instructional Development Paradigms. Englewood Cliffs, NJ: Educational Technology Publications.

Elmer-Dewitt, P. (1994). Battle for the Soul of the Internet. Time, 144(4), 50-6.

Eurich, N.P. (1990). The learning industry: education for adult workers. Princeton, N.J: The Carnegie Foundation for the Advancement of Teaching.

Gery, G. (1991). Electronic performance support systems. New York: Weingarten.

Grabowski, B., Suciati, & Pusch, W. (1990). Social and intellectual value of computer-mediated communications in a graduate community. Educational and Training Technology International, 27(3), 276-83.

Grief, I. (1988). Computer-supported cooperative work: a book of readings. San Mateo, CA: Kaufman.

Hiltz, S.R. (1986). The "virtual classroom": using computer mediated communication for university teaching. Journal of Communication, 36(2), 95-104.

Hiltz, S.R. (1990). Evaluating the virtual classroom. In L.M. Harasim (ed.), Online education: perspectives on a new environment, 133-83. New York: Praeger.

Horn, R. (1989). Mapping hypertext. Lexington, MA: The Lexington Institute.

Kaye, A.R. (1992). Collaborative learning through computer conferencing: the Najadn papers. New York: Springer.

Lewis, J.H., & Romiszowski, A.J. (1995). Networking and the learning organization. Paper presented at the IDLA Conference on "Networking into the 21st Century." Indonesia, October 1995.

Khan, B.H. (1996). Web-based instruction. Englewood Cliffs, NJ: Educational Technology Publications.

Nicoll, D. (1987). Vocational teaching at a distance: the New Zealand perspective. Paper delivered at the UNISA Conference on Distance Education, Pretoria, South Africa, May 1987.

Rajasingham, L., Nicoll, D., & Romiszowski, A.J. (1992). The Technical Open Polytechnic, New Zealand. In G. Rumble & J. Oliveira (eds.), Vocational education at a distance. London: Kogan Page.

Romiszowski, A.J. (1993). Telecommunications in training. In ASTD handbook of training technology, American Society for Training and Development (ASTD).

Romiszowski, A.J., & Chang, E. (1992). Hypertext's contribution to computer-mediated communication: in search of an instructional model. In M. Giardina (ed.), Interactive multimedia learning environments. Berlin: Springer.

Romiszowski, A.J., & Corso, M. (1990). Computer mediated seminars and case studies. Paper presented at the 15th World Conference on Distance Education, Caracas, Venezuela. International Council for Distance Education (ICDE).

Romiszowski, A.J., & Jost, K., & Chang, E. (1990). Computer-mediated communication: a hypertext approach to structuring distance seminars. In Proceedings of the 32nd Annual ADCIS International Conference. Association for the Development of Computer-based Instructional Systems (ADCIS).

Romiszowski, A.J., & Lewis, J. (1995). Instructional systems design and development for a networked society. Paper presented at the IDLN First International Symposium "Networking into the 21st Century." Yogyakarta, Indonesia.

Romiszowski, A.J. & Mason, R. (1996). Computer mediated communication. In D.H. Jonassen (ed.), Handbook of Research for Educational Communications and Technology. New York: Macmillan.

Rumble, G., & Oliveira, J. (1992). Vocational education at a distance: international perspectives. London: Kogan Page.

Daniel/Stevens (pages 156-167)

Daniel, JS (1996) *Mega-universities and Knowledge Media: Technology Strategies for Higher Education,* London, Kogan Page

Daniel, JS (1997) Implications of New Technologies for the International Baccalaureate, *IB World*, to be published

Daniel, JS & Marquis, C. (1979) Independence and Interaction: Getting the Mixture Right, *Teaching at a Distance,* 14, 29-44

Harasim (pages 181-201)

Bacsich, P. (1997). Re-engineering the Campus with Web and related technology for the Virtual University: Insights from my work in Europe analysed in the context of developments in the US. School of Computing and Management, Sheffield Hallam University, Sheffield, U.K.At http://www.cms.shu.ac.uk/public/events/flish97/bacsich-paper.htm

Ehrmann, S. (1994). Responding to the Triple Challenge: Facing Post-Secondary Education: Accessbility, Quality, Costs. A Report for the Organisation for Economic Cooperation and Development, Centre for Educational Research and Innovation. At http://www.learner.org

Hafner, K and Lyon, M. (1996). *Where Wizards Stay Up Late: The origins of the Internet*. New York: Simon and Shuster.

Feenberg, A. (1993). Building a global network: The WBSI executive education experience. In L. Harasim (Ed.). *Global Networks: Computers and International Communication*. Cambridge, MA: MIT.

Harasim, L., Calvert, T. and Groeneboer, C. (1997). Virtual-U: A Web Based System to Support Collaborative Learning. In B. Khan's, *Web-Based Instruction,* Englewood Cliffs, NJ, Educational Technology Publications.

Harasim, L., Hiltz, R., Teles, L., and Turoff, M. (1995). *Learning Networks: A Field Guide to Teaching & Learning Online.* Cambridge, MA: MIT Press.

Harasim, L. (Ed.). (1993). *Global Networks: Computers and Communication.* Cambridge, MA: MIT Press.

Harasim, L. (1993). Collaborating in Cyberspace: Using Computer Conferences as a Group Learning Environment. *Interactive Learning Environments 3* (2), pp. 119-130.

Harasim, L. (Ed.) (1990). *Online education: Perspectives on a new environment.* New York: Praeger Publishers.

Hiltz, S. R. (1990). Evaluating the virtual classroom. In L. Harasim *ed. Online education: Perspectives on a new environment* (pp. 133-185). New York: Prager Publishers.

Hiltz, S. R. (1993). *The virtual classroom: A new option for learning via computer networking.* Norwood, NJ: Ablex.

Keating, D., and Mustard, J.F. (1993). Social Economic Factors And Human Development. In D. Ross (Ed) Family Security in Insecure Times: National forum on family security. Ottawa, ON.

Knight, P. (1996).Quality in Higher Education and the Assessment of Student Learning. Invited address to the *EECAE 96.*

Mason, R. (1997). *Global Education.* In Press. Institute of Educational Technology, The Open University, U.K.

Mason, R. (1996). Old World Visits New. *Innovations in Education and Training International,* vol. 33, no. 1, pp 68-69.

Riel, M. and Harasim, L. (1994). Research Perspectives on Network Learning Environments. *Journal of Machine-Mediated Learning,* 4(2&3), 91-114.

Scardamalia, M. & Bereiter, C. (1993). Technologies for knowledge-building discourse. *Communications of the ACM, 36(5),* pp. 37-41.

RESOURCES AND WEB SITES

Linda M. Harasim

Web Site Resources

Linda Harasim, School of Communication, Simon Fraser University
http://fas.sfu.ca/telelearn/homepages/harasim/harasim.htm

The Potential of the Web:
http:/www.umuc.edu/iuc/workshop97/

Shaping Cyberspace into Human Space:
http://fas.sfu.ca/0h/css/update/vol6/6.3-harasim.main.html

Tips for Creating Virtual Learning Spaces:
http://fas.sfu.ca/0h/css/update/vol6/6.3-tips-Virtual-Learning.html

Why Computer Conferencing:
http://fas.sfu.ca/0h/css/update/vol6/6.3-Why-comp-conf.html

Improving Economic Management Training: http://www.world-bank.org/html/fpd/technet/mdf/edi-trng/index.htm

Paper for the World Bank's Conference on "Global Knowledge '97: Knowledge for Development in the Information Age", Canada:
http://www.worldbank.org/html/edi/toronto/index.htm

Telelearning, Distance Education,Canadian Resources

The TeleLearning Network of Centres of Excellence:
http://www.telelearn.ca

The Virtual-U:
http://virtual-u.cs.sfu.ca

Canada's SchoolNet:
http://www.schoolnet.ca/

Industry Canada's "Computers for Schools" Program:
http://xinfo.ic.gc.ca/ic-data/cfs/

Canadian Education on the Web:
http://www.oise.utoronto.ca/~mpress/eduweb.html

TACT. bilingual site with educational resources:
http://www.tact.fse.ulaval.ca/

Community Access Program (CAP) for rural Canadian communities:
http://cnet.unb.ca/cap/

Selected School and Teacher Networks

COVIS (http://www.covis.nwu.edu/). Learning Through Collaborative Visualization Project (CoVis) is a community of thousands of students, over one hundred teachers, and dozens of researchers all working together to find new ways to think about and practice science in the classroom. They do this by approaching the learning of science more like the doing of science, and by employing a broad range of communication and collaboration technologies.

The Education Network of Ontario (http://www.enoreo.on.ca/)

National Geographic Kids Network Project (http://science.stark.k12.oh.us/NATGEO.HTML). The National Geographic Kids Network Project is a series of flexible elementary science units that feature cooperative experiments in which students in grades 4-6 share data nationwide through the use of telecommunications. Topics will involve the students in issues of real scientific, social, and geographic significance. The Network project combines basic content from typical school curricula with guided inquiry learning. Kids Network can be used to supplement textbooks and existing materials or to form complete, year-long science courses. Various units, software, and telecommunications are designed by Technical Education Research Centers (TERC).

WebCSILE project (http://csile.oise.utoronto.ca/).CSILE - Computer Supported Intentional Learning Environments is a program designed to help students achieve extraordinary learning by providing supports for thinking and understanding. CSILE is the first network system to provide across-the-curriculum support for collaborative learning and inquiry. CSILE is currently running in over 50 classrooms and several cultural institutions in Canada, the U.S., Europe, Australia, and Japan. It is an integral part of the Schools for Thought program in the U.S. and also one of four beacon technologies being developed for the TeleLearning Network of Centres of Excellence.

Writers in Electronic Residence (http://130.63.218.180:80/WIERhome/). Writers In Electronic Residence (WIER) based at York University in Ontario Canada, connects students across Canada with writers, teachers and one another in an animated exchange of original writing and commentary. The writers, who are all well-known Canadian authors, join classrooms electronically to read and consider the students' work, offer reactions and ideas, and guide discussions between the students. In WIER, technology becomes a catalyst for learning more than a simple tool of production. Students compose their works and responses to the works of others offline before posting their writing in our online conference.

University and Professional Education Courses

Birkbeck College (http://www.cryst.bbk.ac.uk/PPS/index.html). London University.

FUQUA (http://www.fuqua.duke.edu/programs/gemba).

The Learning Network at U.S.A.-based Spectrum Virtual University offers free courses about the Web and the Internet and hands-on learning (http://www.vu.org)

Nova Southeastern Educational Technology (http://www.nova.edu/pet/itde.html)

Ontartio Institute for Studies in Education of the University of Toronto (http://www.oise.on.ca/).

Scotland University of Paisley's OnLine Education. (http://www.online.edu/).

Simon Fraser University's Centre for Distance Education [CDE] (http://www.cde.sfu.ca/), is one of the largest distance education programs in Canada. The CDE's LohnLab for Online Teaching and learning is where instructors can share their experiences in using new pedogogical models for course enhancement and delivery, using Virtual-U.

Télé-Université (http://unitl/teluq.uquebec.ca/~licef/html/teleform.html) is fieldtesting ASDL, ISDN, and ATM applications fo Teleform for distance education.

University of Twente (http://www.to.utwente.nl/ism/online96/campus.htm)

Others mentioned in paper:

Sister Cities (http://www.sister-cities.org/index.html)
I*EARN (http://www.iearn.org/iearn/)

RealAudio (http://www.realaudio.com)

KMI Stadium (http://kmi.open.ac.uk/stadium)

Virtual-U (http://virtual-u.cs.sfu.ca)
Acadia University (http://www.acadiau.ca/)

Globewide Network Academy (http://uu-gna.mit.edu:8001/uu-gna/index.html)

Spectrum Virtual University (http://www.athena.edu)

Phoenix University (http://www.uophx.edu)

IMLearn (http://www.imlearn.com)

Knowledge Online by U.S.-based Jones Education Company (http://www.jec.edu/)

IBM Global Network (http://ike.engr.washington.edu/igc/)

Microsoft Online Institute (MOLI) (http://microsoft.com./uk/channel_resources/online.htm)

Stanford Professional Development Centre : Stanford Online (http://stanford-online.stanford.edu/)

Motorola University (http://www.mot.com/MU/)

CALCampus (http://www.calcampus.com)

Western Governors' Inititative (http://www.westgov.org/smart/vu/vuvision)

Canadian SchoolNet (http://www.schoolnet.ca)

TL-NCE (http://www.telelearn.ca)

The Cartagena Declaration
July 11, 1997

This document is the outcome of the Seminar *Education in the Information Age: An Agenda for Action in Latin America and the Caribbean,* held in July, 1997 in Cartagena, Colombia, and organized by the Inter-American Development Bank (IDB), the Universidad de los Andes, Colombia, and the Global Information Infrastructure Commission (GIIC). In the Seminar, Ministers and representatives of Latin American and Caribbean governments engaged in dialogue and exchange of ideas with leading businesses in the field of information technology as well as with representatives of the IDB and academia. The IDB and the participating education authorities agreed to issue a declaration aimed at 1) highlighting the key role of information technology in education for the region, 2) summing up the main lessons learned, as presented and discussed in the seminar, and 3) issuing guidelines for future action by both governments and the Bank regarding investment in information technology for educational purposes. A draft version was circulated among Ministers of Education of all member countries and subsequently modified according to their suggestions. The final version, to which all parties agreed tacitly or explicitly, follows.

PREAMBLE

The new information technologies will bring major changes in education

New information technologies impact societies in a number of ways. Education and training systems have the responsibility to prepare individuals for the new information society. The new requirements brought about by both the new information era and the new information technologies include equipping individuals with the information, knowledge and skills to understand, effectively operate, and productively contribute to society.

The impact of the new information technologies on the ways and means to convey education and training is pervasive. On the one hand they introduce new ways and possibilities to deal with information, which in turn impact the nature and speed of communications and learning. On the other hand, they present alternative systems and tools for teaching and learning. Effective dealing with the new information technologies requires more than simply adding new subjects or new hardware and software to schools and training institutions. While some of the requirements of the new information society may not necessarily require the use of technology in the teaching process, there are many situations in which such use becomes not only appropriate, but also mandatory.

New information technologies have profound cost implications. They may contribute to decrease unit costs when used as alternatives to conventional schools-as in distance education-or to improve the efficiency of the use of scarce resources when used as a management tool. But they may also imply increased costs when used to improve quality, expand or enrich existing educational processes. Thus, under a situation of scarce resources, it becomes critical both to choose the appropriate niche for using technology in education and to choose the appropriate technology.

Education in Latin America remains a problem, not a solution

Education in Latin America has made great progress in the last four decades. Public and private investments in education have been increasing and vary from 3 to 4.5 percent of national GNPs in the various countries in the region. Access has been significantly improved and is almost universal for the majority of the compulsory school-age population. Secondary education is expanding and access to higher education has significantly improved.

Overall, however, major problems still remain. Curricula are outmoded. Student learning in primary and secondary is rather limited in relation to expectations. Repetition rates are very high and drop-out rates are still a major problem in many countries. Teaching did not become an attractive career. The financing of education, the mechanisms of resource allocation and spending scarce resources are hardly adequate to maintain the present levels of expansion, not to mention the need to promote significant improvements in quality. Differences in access and equity are greater within than between countries, thus contributing to widening the gap between those who will and those who will not benefit from education and economic development.

Differences also exist in the access of schools to infra-structures which are necessary for the effective use of the new information technologies.

Responding to the challenges of bringing the new information technologies to education

The experience with the introduction of new information technologies in education in both developed and developing countries is relatively recent and rather limited. The results are mixed. Moreover, what works in developed countries does not necessarily work in the developing ones.

In the developed countries the new information technologies are being introduced in a context in which universal education is already in place, schools have adequately trained teachers, telecommunications infra-structures exist, and resources for instructional materials represent around 10 percent of total expenditures in schools. With the exception of Distance Learning Universities which are used to expand access, new technologies, especially computers, are being used to improve quality and enrich the curricula.

In the developing countries of Latin America, the conditions are different. Distance education may be called upon to fill the gaps of access and of inadequately trained teachers. The introduction of new technologies needs to take into consideration the limitations of infra-structure and other resources which are necessary for a successful and sustained use.

The experience of the Region with the use of some technologies, particularly those which substitute scarce resources—rather than present additional demands on such scarce resources—has been reasonably successful. These include a number of distance learning programs using radio, television or correspondence schools, as well as robust materials using sophisticated techniques of instructional design. In many instances of success such technologies were used outside the constraints of the formal systems of education and training, thus maximizing the effects of scale and intensive utilization of inputs which would otherwise be in place. The use of computers in Latin America Schools has been more limited and recent. Yet, there are encouraging experiments in a few countries. Such efforts were more successful in places where infrastructure and the necessary equipment was already in place, sometimes as a result of well-targeted government policies for technology in education. Given that equity and access are still major challenges for educational systems in some countries, the technologies which replace or supplement such scarce resources such as television may be more effective and efficient than technologies used in a manner which require a higher and/or more intensive (and costly) use of such scarce resources.

Moving from small scale to larger scale projects is not a simple or logical next step and requires careful planning and implementation. Even projects which succeed when implemented on a small scale face different challenges when the scale changes. Thus, the probability of success of mega projects and other uniform or broad-scale initiatives is not predicted by highly promising and visible results in the beginning stages.

Experience shows that systems that were able to successfully introduce computers had to revise curricula and learning objectives for students, developing higher quality instructional materials which foster interaction and higher order cognitive skills. They also had to prepare teachers to adopt participatory, group and student-centered methodologies, as well as use evaluation strategies compatible with the learning objectives. As much as it is desirable to introduce each of these elements in an orderly and logical sense, the realities of implementation may force second-best solutions.

Particularly in the case of distance education, the private sector plays a major role in the development, provision and management of inputs which are critical for the effective introduction and dissemination of technologies in the schools. These include the provision of infrastructures and networks, instructional programs and software, broadcast systems and programs as well as partnership, technical and financial support for R&D, educational reform and public schools. The need of the private sector to remain competitive and associated technological breakthroughs have contributed to dramatic cost reductions which render access to information related hardware and services more affordable. Partnerships with the private sector also contribute to improve management and to the feasibility of implementing more ambitious projects. Parents and teachers organization as well as NGO's have played a major role in supporting program to introduce computers in schools. Public policies should encourage these partnerships.

Ideas and plans are not sufficient. The experiences of both developed and Latin American countries suggest a number of common features in computer projects that were successfully implemented. They include first, a clear vision of education and of the requirements of the new information age. Second, while it is not appropriate to postulate pre-defined trajectories and practical constraints may impose different sequences, successful policies are often the result of successful projects started at the grass-roots level, and based on accumulated learning about what works under local circumstances. Successful projects, in general, were developed to address concrete needs, i. e., projects which have been pulled by the schools rather than pushed from the outside. Attempts to leap frog such steps decrease the chance of success. Third, they require careful and detailed planning. Fourth, they require adequate and stable sources of funding for equipment and infrastructure (usually 40 to 50 percent of total budgets), recurrent resources for teacher training (usually 30 percent) and for maintenance and updating of hardware and software (usually 10 to 20 percent). Fifth, they require changes in administration, curricula and methodology. Sixth, they require a minimum set of rules and standards associated with lots of freedom for local initiatives, adaptation and experimentation. Seventh, they require the involvement and commitment of teachers and principals. Eighth, they involve parental and social understanding and approval. Finally, they require permanent evaluation and feedback to improve the system.

RECOMMENDATIONS

The new information age requires governments of all countries to establish policies which will ensure access to and competence in the use of such technologies. National policies for the new information technologies include taking into consideration the goals, content, methods and delivery systems. Over time such new policies may introduce profound, if not radical changes in education and training practices.

Such policies should take into consideration the deployment of compatible and affordable infrastructures, the development of a new vision for education, a sense of direction, the establishment of clear goals and adequate strategies to reach them, the permanent monitoring and evaluations of results.

Policies to introduce new technologies for education and training must take into consideration the characteristics, culture and possibilities of each country. They require clear cut goals and targets to be achieved. At the same time they require governments to reach a difficult equilibrium between a minimum set of common rules and standards with sufficient room for schools and other institutions to experiment with ideas and adapt general rules to concrete situations without losing focus and a sense of priority.

In view of the realities, the needs and the potential of the New Information Technologies for the future of education in the region, the following recommendations may be considered by countries and the IDB.

RECOMMENDATIONS FOR COUNTRIES

Countries in the region should create an adequate framework and when appropriate, develop national policies for information technology likely to promote educational reform. Such framework and policies should include:

A. Concerning Information Infrastructure

- Particularly in the case of privately operated infrastructure, establish a positive business climate and clear policy directions to foster the development of widespread, efficient communication networks to facilitate the access and utilization of affordable information systems.

- Interconnect information and communications networks, and ensure their inter-operability through the promotion of market-led standards and technologies.

- Create stable rules and transparent procedures which are the prerequisites to enhance the confidence of potential investors both domestic and foreign.

- Promote and encourage joint investments in basic scientific research and development between governments and private industry.

B. Concerning education information technology policies

- Develop ambitious but realistic plans, goals, standards and targets to meet the requirements of the new information age. Such plans should include the new contents and skills to be developed at the various levels, the human and technical competencies required to support the new curricula, the technological choices concerning equipment and other aspects and the requirements to ensure connectivity with the various sources of information. Last but not least, the careful and recurrent preparation of teachers in essential.

- Set up clear priorities for the use of information technology (IT) that foster access and equity in the education systems and the judicious choice of technologies which lead to attaining such goals for a broad clientele.

- Support the development of national capabilities in the critical areas of instructional design and adaptation of existing training materials and educational software.

- Facilitate and promote partnerships between educational systems, schools and the private sector, and promote regional cooperation and exchange of experience and information between research groups within the respective countries and worldwide.

- Stimulate international cooperation by means of an increased flow of information and software, as well as programs of distance education and other learning opportunities. Among the tools to attain these objectives are the promotion of unobtrusive mechanisms for accreditation of institutions and programs and certification of individuals.

- Encourage local experimentation and research to ensure that each country masters of all major aspects of dealing with new information technology, as well support the development of networks of teachers, researchers and providers of key resources and inputs.

- Monitor the implementation of policies and plans and assess the results obtained.

RECOMMENDATIONS FOR THE INTER-AMERICAN DEVELOPMENT BANK

To maintain its leadership in promoting new information technologies for educational development, the IDB should ensure that individual country projects approved by its Board contribute to and reflect consistent national policies. Such policies should contain the essential ingredients for success, focus on the right educational priorities and set feasible and realistic targets. For that purpose it is recommended that the IDB:

- Fund IT based projects, including for the deployment of infrastructures, as well as the acquisition and dissemination of hardware and software.

- Set up rigorous analysis of the projects and proposals to ensure their consistency with the educational policies and priorities of the IDB and the member countries.

- Provide technical assistance to help countries design appropriate IT and educational IT policies

- Support the development of clearinghouses, task-forces and other capabilities to promote data collection, monitor progress, evaluation and exchange of information about IT and its uses in the region, to ensure access to all countries to the available information, knowledge, experience and evaluation.

- Initiate, lead, facilitate and/or support the development of partnerships between countries as well as between public and private sector organizations (such as the Global Information Infrastructure Commission).